# Why They Left

Listening to Those Who Have Left Churches of Christ

Published by Gospel Advocate Co.
1006 Elm Hill Pike, Nashville, TN 37210
www.gospeladvocate.com

ISBN 10: 0-89225-593-5
ISBN 13: 978-0-89225-593-1

# Dedication

This book is lovingly dedicated in general to the many thousands of faithful members who have not left the Churches of Christ. They have patiently stayed in local congregations in spite of many human imperfections while working to improve things. Many of these families have roots that go back several generations in Churches of Christ. They have demonstrated that it is possible to pass on their faith from generation to generation. Now, however, the focus must turn to those who will come after us.

My wife, Maydell, and I have three children and eight grandchildren. Two of our granddaughters are now married. So there are now 10 in that generation of the Yeakley family. This book is specifically dedicated to them: to the children of Mark and Kimberlee: Ryan, Rachel and her husband Zach Sewell; to the children of Steven and Shelley: Stuart, Stanton and Sheldon; to the children of Rebecca and Gene Vinzant: Sarah and her husband Michael Crouch, Anna and John. Those grandchildren have roots that go back at least six generations in Churches of Christ.

The two most important things that parents can give children are roots and wings. These grandchildren now have both. My prayer for them is that they will remember their spiritual roots and use their wings in a way that serves the cause of Jesus Christ. This is also my prayer for the children and grandchildren of all those in Churches of Christ with all the generations that are yet to come.

The leader of some young troublemakers thought that he had found a way to prove a wise old man to be wrong. He caught a bird and held it in his hands. He told his followers, "I will show the bird to the wise old man and ask if the bird is living or dead. If he says that the bird is dead, I will open my hands and let the bird go free. If he says that the bird is living, I will crush it to death. Either way I will prove the wise old man to be wrong."

So the young troublemakers went to the wise old man and their leader showed the bird held in his hands. He asked "Is this bird alive or dead?"

The wise old man answered, "My Son, it is as you will, for it is in your hands."

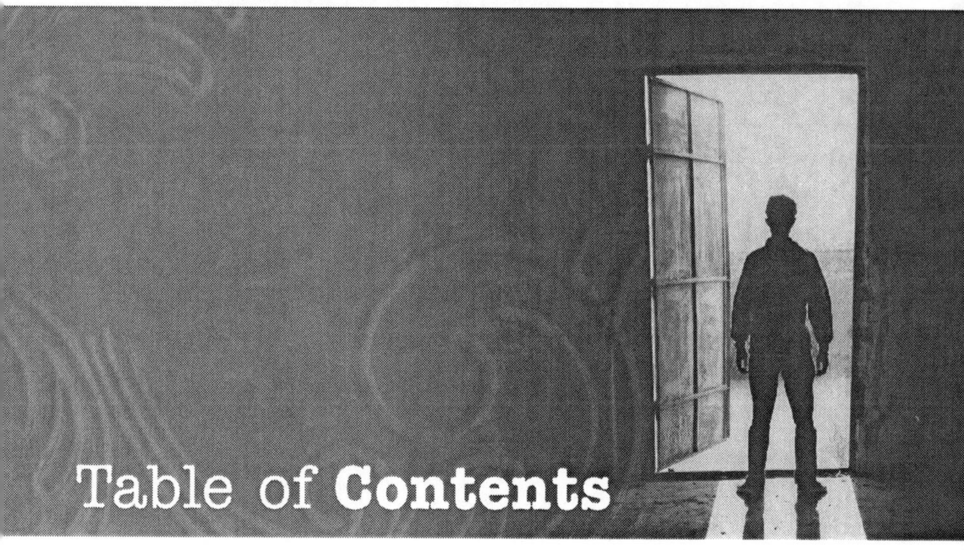

# Table of **Contents**

# Foreword

Some of my most cherished memories revolve around the Rosen Heights Church of Christ in Fort Worth, Texas. My uncles, J. Willard Morrow and Bennett Morrow, were preachers for the congregation as far back as I can remember. Each Sunday morning at some point in the worship service, there was what we called the "Children's Song" when all the little ones would go to the front of the auditorium and usually sing "When We All Get to Heaven" with the entire congregation singing along with us. To this day, more than 70 years later, I silently give thanks to God for the Rosen Heights Church of Christ each time the church sings this song. I will always love that church for the influence it has had on my life as a disciple of Jesus Christ, a minister of the word, a foreign missionary, a university Bible professor and administrator, and Christian writer and editor. As a matter of fact, I have had a lifelong love affair with the Church of Christ wherever I have found it throughout the world.

This love affair, therefore, has made it difficult for me to understand why anyone would want to leave the Church of Christ. When I have had personal conversations with some who have left, I have been stunned to hear them describe the churches in which they grew up or the churches they chose to leave. Their experiences were so different from mine that I found it difficult to believe we were even talking about the same church. I have heard others who stayed and did not leave express feelings similar to mine. Why would anyone want to leave Churches of Christ?

Flavil Yeakley and I became friends after we both had been preaching for a number of years. It has been a special pleasure to work with him as a colleague at Harding University in Searcy, Ark.; attend the College Church of Christ together with our wives who are also friends; team together on some writing projects; and frequently discuss our mutual joys and concerns about happenings within Churches of Christ.

I have concluded from our countless conversations that Flavil and I both have many sweet memories about childhood religious experiences that were intertwined with loving family and friends who encouraged our commitment to Christ. At the same time, we are not naïve. Growing up as we both did within families that were on the front line of local churches and brotherhood issues, we know that we have never been able to become precisely the church that existed in the mind of God from before the creation of the world. We know from years of personal experience that every congregation can have its problems and challenges – even sometimes a dark underbelly – that should not exist. Despite its shortcomings, we both love the Church of Christ because of what it stands for and because of its desire to follow the teachings of God's Word and imitate the example of Jesus Christ.

Flavil Yeakley, however, likes to get to the bottom of things. He wants to know what has motivated some people to leave Churches of Christ so those of us who have stayed can make whatever corrections that may need to be made, clarify any misunderstandings that exist, and do a better job of presenting ideas and practices that we believe are non-negotiable.

In this book, numerous character traits of Flavil Yeakley come to the surface. He is courageous, full of curiosity, open-minded, committed to truth, willing to listen and learn, and a peacemaker. He has made a genuine effort to find out from anonymous respondents why they left the Church of Christ. Although their answers are sometimes difficult for a lover of the Church of Christ to hear, Flavil pays close attention and offers comments that are thoughtful and kind. He deals with subjects like instrumental music, the role of women, church leadership, marriage and divorce, and other serious doctrinal questions such as who will be saved and who will be lost.

Even though we may not fully agree with every one of Flavil Yeakley's answers, or we may wish he had said something in a slightly different way at times, we should all be grateful that he has opened a dialog with people who used to be a part of Churches of Christ and chose to leave. They are our sons and daughters, brothers and sisters, aunts and uncles, friends and associates. We continue to love them. Our prayer is that Flavil Yeakley's efforts in this book will contribute to reconciliation and the unity for which Jesus prayed.

*– Howard W. Norton*

*President, Baxter Institute, Tegucigalpa, Honduras*

# Preface

The study reported in this book has its limitations and its strengths. If it were possible to do a random sample of those who have left Churches of Christ, we could know how much confidence we could have that the sample was truly representative of all those who have left Churches of Christ. This survey was not like that. Its greatest strength, however, is in the richness of data produced. My somewhat educated guess is that the reasons given in this study for leaving Churches of Christ are not very different from what we would find if we could interview all those who have left Churches of Christ. Such interviews with the whole population of former members would not likely generate any new categories of reasons. The way to judge the accuracy in this kind of study is to compare the reasons these former members give for leaving Churches of Christ with what you have observed among people you have known who have left Churches of Christ or what you have observed in various congregations.

This study is a report of some reasons given by some former members explaining why they left Churches of Christ at some time in the past. That is history – not prophecy. It tells a little about what was. It does not tell what is now or what will be in the future. A different kind of research will be needed to focus on present trends and project what may happen in the future. I do not know of any reliable data from studies being done. There is, however, some anecdotal evidence that church leaders should consider seriously.

People who work with the current generation of high school and college-age members of the Churches of Christ are reporting that a majority of them do not expect to remain in Churches of Christ after they graduate and are more independent – that is after they are no longer being supported by their parents. Some who teach at Christian colleges and universities report that a majority of the Bible majors in some of their classes do not expect to stay in Churches of Christ after they graduate. More research will be needed to see if these anecdotal reports accurately represent a larger group of members.

In this book you will read what some people who have left Churches of Christ say about their reasons for leaving. If you respond to their stories in the way I did, you may wonder what you would have done if you had been in their situation. I have never been in their situation. If I had been, I might have had options they did not have. I think that I would make a serious attempt to change things before deciding that I had to leave. I live in a county with more than 30 Churches of Christ. If I could not change things in the church where I am a member, I have plenty of other congregations where I could go. If there were no other congregations within reasonable driving distance from where I life, I think that I would plant another congregation. But I know from experience how difficult church planting is.

I was the first full-time church-supported minister in three new churches and helped three other mission churches become self-supporting. As I look back on these domestic mission, church-planting efforts, I am amazed at how much God was able to do in spite of me and all the mistakes I made.

Starting a new congregation is not a viable option for most members of the Churches of Christ. Transferring membership to another area congregation is not an option for people in places where there is only one Church of Christ within reasonable driving distance. Moving a family in order to find a better congregation might not be a viable alternative. Perhaps going to a Christian Church with the "instrumental brethren" or to an independent community-type church is the least objectionable alternative for some people. It is not for me to say. God did not appoint me as the judge of these people who left Churches of Christ.

It is not my purpose to condemn the people who responded to the "Why I Left Churches of Christ" survey. My hope is that church leaders will learn important lessons from listening to those who have left so that they can do a better job of ministering to those who have not left.

Chapter 1

# About Churches of Christ

This book is about Churches of Christ in the United States.[1] To be more specific, it is about some former members of this fellowship who accepted an invitation to take an open-ended online survey called "Why I Left Churches of Christ." This book is written with the assumption that most of the readers will be present or former members of the Churches of Christ. It is likely, however, that some members of other religious groups may read this book to see what lessons they might learn and apply in their churches. For that reason, it seems necessary to begin with some basic information about Churches of Christ. This introduction may be needed even by some who have been members of the Churches of Christ for many years.

## An Introduction to the Churches of Christ

Will Rogers once said, "I belong to no organized party. I am a Democrat." In that same spirit, I could say, "I belong to no organized religious group. I am a member of the Churches of Christ." Although Churches of Christ are similar in many ways to various Protestant denominations, there are important differences. Churches of Christ exist and function as an informal fellowship of independent congregations with no formal written creed.

They have no central governing body or organizational headquarters with the power to impose conformity. That being the case, informed observers find it remarkable that more than 76.1 percent of the congregations with 87.4 percent of the members are similar enough to one another that no significant barriers to fellowship exist among them.[2] The rest include several groups whose fellowship is limited by some doctrine or practice. "Mutual Edification" churches oppose the practice of having full-time church-supported preachers. "One Cup" congregations oppose the use of individual communion cups. "Non-Class" churches do not believe it is proper to divide the assembly into the traditional kinds of Sunday school classes. "Non-Institutional" churches are opposed to a sponsoring church method of cooperation, church support of children's homes and any other kind of "institutions." Although members of the congregations listed in the directory *Churches of Christ in the United States* do not agree on everything, they are similar enough to one another that they see themselves as a group. The churches listed are those that want to be listed. Those identified with a character code (Non-Institutional, Non-Class, One Cup, etc.) are so identified because they want that information about them to be known.

The limited fellowship groups have many things in common with the "mainstream" congregations. They all practice immersion for the remission of sins. They have weekly observance of the Lord's Supper. Historically, they all have roots in the Stone-Campbell Restoration Movement. Barton Stone and Alexander Campbell would not have wanted this movement to be named after them, and some of their heirs today would prefer that we just call this "The Restoration Movement." Honesty compels us, however, to acknowledge that other religious movements at least claimed to be restoring something important from the New Testament pattern. The Puritans, Anabaptist and Holiness denominations sought to restore moral purity. The Pentecostal denominations seek to restore miraculous gifts of the Holy Spirit that were present in the early church – such as tongues, supernatural healing and casting out demons.

## An Introduction to the Stone-Campbell Restoration Movement

The focus of the movement led by Barton Stone, Alexander Campbell and other such pioneers was primarily on restoring New Testament doctrines concerning salvation, the organization of local churches, and worship assembly practices. Their emphasis on restoring New Testament Christianity was so strong that this became the only religious movement commonly identified by the title "The Restoration Movement."

Three of the largest Christian religious groups in the United States have historical roots in the Stone-Campbell Restoration Movement. Table 1.1 lists the 14 largest Christian fellowships – those with one million or more adherents. Church statisticians use the term "adherents" for all of the fully confirmed communicant members plus their children not yet baptized or baptized as infants but not yet confirmed. In Table 1.1, these 14 groups are ranked by the reported number of adherents starting with the largest group, the Catholic Church. The three groups at the bottom of this table are heirs of the Stone-Campbell Restoration Movement.

## Table 1.1

Major Christian Religious Bodies in the United States Ranked by Number of Adherents in 2000

| Religious Bodies | Adherents |
|---|---|
| Catholic Church | 62,035,042 |
| Southern Baptist Convention | 19,881,467 |
| United Methodist Church | 10,350,629 |
| Evangelical Lutheran Church in America | 5,113,418 |
| Church of Jesus Christ of Latter-day Saints (Mormon) | 4,224,026 |
| Presbyterian Church (USA) | 3,141,566 |
| Assemblies of God | 2,561,998 |
| Lutheran Church (Missouri Synod) | 2,521,062 |
| Episcopal Church | 2,314,758 |
| American Baptist Church in the USA | 1,767,462 |
| United Church of Christ | 1,698,918 |
| Churches of Christ | 1,645,584 |
| Christian Churches and Churches of Christ | 1,439,253 |
| Christian Church (Disciples of Christ) | 1,017,784 |

Most people in America are familiar with the 10 largest denominations listed in this table. The similarity of names for the last four groups may be confusing. The United Church of Christ was formed in 1957 when the Evangelical and Reformed Church merged with the Congregational Christian Church (heirs of the Puritans). In 1931, the Congregational

Christian Church had merged with the Christian Denomination in America, a group that had roots in early restoration efforts by Abner Jones and Elias Smith in New England and James O'Kelly in Virginia. But heirs of these restoration efforts did not join the movement by Barton Stone, Alexander Campbell and other Restoration Movement pioneers. So despite the names being similar, this group has little historical connection with the Churches of Christ. The United Church of Christ was in the news a great deal during the 2008 presidential election. It was President Barack Obama's religious affiliation until his pastor, Jeremiah Wright, became too much of a political embarrassment.

## Major Divisions in the Stone-Campbell Restoration Movement

The last three religious groups listed in Table 1.1 share historical roots in the Stone-Campbell Restoration Movement. In the early days of this movement, the designations "Disciples of Christ," "Christian Churches" and "Churches of Christ" were all used in reference to the same congregations. In the period following the Civil War, some of the churches started using instrumental music in congregational worship assemblies. Churches that opposed this practice became known almost exclusively as "Churches of Christ." Most of the churches that favored instrumental music became known as "Christian Churches."

The U.S. Census Bureau used to publish reference books called *Religious Bodies* in the middle of each census decade. In the 1800s, all of the congregations of the Stone-Campbell Restoration Movement were reported under the designation "Christian Churches." The 1906 edition of *Religious Bodies* was the first in which Churches of Christ and Christian Churches were reported as two separate religious groups, although the actual division had come in the latter part of the 19th century. In the first half of the 20th century, the Christian Churches differed on several issues:

- Open Membership: Accepting people who had never been immersed for the remission of sins on a simple transfer of membership;
- Church Federation: Participation in the National Council of Churches and other such groups;
- The Ecumenical Movement: An effort to merge denominational organizations;

- Liberal Theology: Questioning the full inspiration and authority of the Scriptures, the virgin birth of Jesus, miracles, etc.; and
- Restructure: Leaders of the progressive wing of the Christian Churches had reached the conclusion that the Restoration Plea had not produced the church union they were seeking. They became participants in the efforts to merge denominational organizations. By the 1950s, it had become clear that the Christian Churches could not fully participate in the Ecumenical Movement unless they had a central denominational headquarters that could speak for all of their congregations. That is when the Christian Church (Disciples of Christ) was organized. Note the singular usage in the word "Church." This was no longer an informal fellowship of independent congregations. It was now fully organized as a denomination.

A majority of the Christian Churches refused to participate in the Restructure plan. All of these congregations used instrumental music in their worship assemblies, and that set them apart from the Churches of Christ that did not use instrumental music. But around half of the instrumental congregations used the designation "Churches of Christ." Now in almanacs, yearbooks and in their directories, this fellowship uses the designation "Christian Churches and Churches of Christ." Except for the instrumental music issue and the approach to Bible interpretation that supports it, the two groups are very similar. In fact, the differences between these two fellowships are not as great as the differences within each group. To a statistician, that would mean that these two are really one body separated by reason of conscience. In this one body: some congregations use instrumental music, but more do not; most have Bible classes, but some do not; most use individual communion cups, but a few do not, etc. Functionally, however, the a cappella and instrumental fellowships have been almost totally isolated from one another for more than 100 years.

Table 1.2 lists the 14 largest Christian religious fellowships in the United States. This time, however, the number of adherents is compared with the average attendance reported for each group. The ranking is by attendance as a percentage of the reported number of adherents. Relative places in the ranking were estimated for three groups. The Catholic Church and the Mormons never report attendance figures. Christian Churches and

Churches of Christ usually collect attendance figures, but for some reason these were not included in the 2000 study. The results show a dramatic difference between Churches of Christ and most of the other church bodies.

## Table 1.2

Major Christian Religious Groups in the United States Ranked by Attendance as a Percentage of the Reported Number of Adherents

| Religious Group | Adherents | Attendance | Percent |
|---|---|---|---|
| Churches of Christ | 1,645,584 | 1,256,845 | 76.4 |
| Christian Churches and Churches of Christ | 1,439,253 | ? | ? |
| Assemblies of God | 2,561,998 | 1,623,889 | 63.4 |
| Church of Jesus Christ of Latter-day Saints | 4,224,026 | ? | ? |
| Presbyterian Church (USA) | 3,141,566 | 1,303,216 | 41.5 |
| Lutheran Church (Missouri Synod) | 2,521,062 | 968,073 | 38.4 |
| American Baptist Churches, USA | 1,767,462 | 661,225 | 37.4 |
| Episcopal Church | 2,314,756 | 836,143 | 36.1 |
| United Methodist Church | 10,350,629 | 3,487,039 | 33.7 |
| United Church of Christ | 1,698,918 | 568,552 | 33.5 |
| Evangelical Lutheran Church in America | 5,113,418 | 1,560,712 | 30.5 |
| Southern Baptist Convention | 19,881,467 | 5,535,891 | 27.8 |
| Christian Church (Disciples of Christ) | 1,017,784 | 265,282 | 26.1 |
| Catholic Church | 62,035,042 | ? | ? |

## The Need to Correct Perceptions

People from other religious groups are not the only ones who may have distorted perceptions regarding the Churches of Christ. Many members of the Churches of Christ grew up in very small congregations and had little contact with other congregations. Among all the congregations of the Churches of Christ in the United States, 34.6 percent have fewer than 50 members; 63.3 percent have fewer than 100 members. Many of the members know only their local church and perhaps a few others in the area or a few others where they have lived in the past. But they do not see the big picture. Many members of the Churches of Christ grew up with the perception that they belonged to a very small unimportant religious group that was badly divided and rapidly declining. Many believe they are virtually alone.[3]

That is what happened to the prophet Elijah in 1 Kings 19:1-18. He thought that he was the only one left who served Jehovah. He was so discouraged that he wanted to die. But Elijah's perceptions were not accurate. God told him that there were still 7,000 who "have not bowed to Baal" (v. 18). Knowing that he was not alone gave Elijah the courage to return to the work God had given him to do. In a similar way, some members of the Churches of Christ need to know that they are not alone.

In the preparation of the reference book *Religious Congregations and Membership in the United States 2000*, the Association of Statisticians of American Religious Bodies (ASARB) had full reports from 135 religious groups and 14 others that reported only the number and location of congregations. In addition, ASARB had addresses for around 100 very small denominations that did not participate. That study identified around 250 separate religious groups in America that are identified as "Christian." There may, however, be some justification for focusing primarily on the 14 largest. Each of those listed in Table 1.1, has 1 million or more adherents. Together these 14 groups account for more than 90 percent of the adherents in all Christian fellowships in the nation. I am not interested in promoting denominational competition or sectarian pride. But instead of feeling discouraged because 11 denominations have more adherents than the Churches of Christ, perhaps it would be more realistic to understand that around 238 denominations have fewer adherents than the Churches of Christ.

Table 1.3 lists the 14 largest religious groups in America ranked by the number of congregations. Only the three largest denominations have more congregations than Churches of Christ.

## Table 1.3

Major Christian Religious Bodies in the United States Ranked by Number of Congregations in 2000

| **Religious Bodies** | **Congregations** |
|---|---|
| Southern Baptist Convention | 41,514 |
| United Methodist Church | 35,721 |
| Catholic Church | 21,721 |
| Churches of Christ | 13,027 |
| Assemblies of God | 11,880 |
| Church of Jesus Christ of Latter-day Saints | 11,515 |
| Presbyterian Church (USA) | 11,106 |

| | |
|---|---|
| Evangelical Lutheran Church in America | 10,739 |
| Episcopal Church | 7,314 |
| Lutheran Church (Missouri Synod) | 6,088 |
| United Church of Christ | 5,863 |
| Christian Churches and Churches of Christ | 5,471 |
| Christian Church (Disciples of Christ) | 3,339 |
| American Baptist Churches in the USA | 1,867 |

Churches of Christ seem to be concentrated in just a few states. Table 1.4 shows the 13 states where Churches of Christ have a higher than average concentration of adherents, members and congregations. More than one-third of these are located in just two states: Texas and Tennessee. More than half are located in these two states plus Alabama, Arkansas and Oklahoma. More than 70 percent are in the 13 states shown in Table 1.4. This distribution is a good argument in favor of more domestic church-planting mission work. The 37 other states have more than three-fourths of the nation's population but less than one-third of the adherents, members and congregations among the Churches of Christ.

## Table 1.4

Distribution of Churches of Christ in States With a Relatively High Concentration of Adherents, Members and Congregations

| **Cumulative** | | |
|---|---|---|
| **States** | **Percent** | **Percent** |
| Texas | 22.4 | 22.4 |
| Tennessee | 13.2 | 35.6 |
| Alabama | 7.2 | 42.8 |
| Arkansas | 5.3 | 48.1 |
| Oklahoma | 4.9 | 53.0 |
| Kentucky | 3.6 | 56.6 |
| Georgia | 3.2 | 59.8 |
| Missouri | 2.7 | 62.5 |
| Mississippi | 2.6 | 65.1 |
| Indiana | 2.1 | 67.2 |
| West Virginia | 1.5 | 68.7 |
| Kansas | 1.1 | 69.8 |
| New Mexico | 1.1 | 70.9 |

The level of concentration shown in Table 1.4 is not unusual when compared with other religious groups in the United States. Church statisticians regard the number of counties in which a religious group has a presence as being one good indication of how dispersed that group is throughout the nation. Table 1.5 provides such a comparison. When this study was done in 2000, there were 3,141 counties or county-equivalents in the United States. Churches of Christ had a presence in more counties than all but four denominations. Furthermore, three of those denominations are the largest in the nation; one would expect them to be in a large number of counties. The only other denomination that had a presence in more counties than the Churches of Christ was the Assemblies of God.

## Table 1.5

Major Christian Religious Bodies in the United States Ranked by the Number of Counties in Which Each Had a Presence

| Religious Bodies | Number of Counties in Which Each Group Had a Presence |
|---|---|
| United Methodist Church | 3,003 |
| Catholic Church | 2,987 |
| Southern Baptist Convention | 2,670 |
| Assemblies of God | 2,616 |
| Churches of Christ | 2,429 |
| Presbyterian Church (USA) | 2,377 |
| Episcopal Church | 2,118 |
| Church of Jesus Christ of Latter-day Saints (Mormon) | 1,802 |
| Lutheran Church (Missouri Synod) | 1,801 |
| Evangelical Lutheran Church in America | 1,756 |
| Christian Churches and Churches of Christ | 1,600 |
| Christian Church (Disciples of Christ) | 1,290 |
| United Church of Christ | 1,229 |
| American Baptist Churches in the USA | 1,111 |

Another factor to consider is how evenly a religious group is distributed throughout the nation in relation to its size. One would expect the very large religious groups to have congregations in many counties. It is not unusual that the Catholic Church with more than 62 million adherents would have a presence in almost 3,000 counties. It also would be expected that the largest Protestant denomination, the Southern Baptist Convention, with more than 40,000 congregations that report having almost 20 million adherents, would have a presence in a large number of counties. In fact, they report having a presence in more than 2,600 counties.[4] But for some purposes it is important to have a way of comparing the 14 largest Christian religious bodies in America (those with 1 million or more adherents) in regard to how evenly they are spread throughout the nation in relation to their size. One indication of this is the average number of adherents per county in which each group has a presence. The lower that number, the more evenly that group is distributed throughout the nation in relation to its size. Table 1.6 shows that comparison.

## Table 1.6

Major Christian Religious Bodies in the United States Ranked by the Average Number of Adherents Per County in Which That Group Has a Presence as an Indication of How Evenly that Group is Spread Throughout the Nation in Relation to the Size of Each Group

| **Religious Bodies** | **Average Number of Adherents Per County** |
|---|---:|
| Churches of Christ | 678 |
| Christian Church (Disciples of Christ) | 789 |
| Christian Churches and Churches of Christ | 900 |
| Assemblies of God | 979 |
| Episcopal Church | 1,093 |
| Presbyterian Church (USA) | 1,322 |
| United Church of Christ | 1,382 |
| Lutheran Church (Missouri Synod) | 1,400 |
| American Baptist Churches in the USA | 1,591 |
| Church of Jesus Christ of Latter-day Saints | 2,344 |
| Evangelical Lutheran Church in America | 2,912 |
| United Methodist Church | 3,447 |
| Southern Baptist Convention | 7,446 |
| Catholic Church | 20,768 |

Another perception needs to be corrected. Some critics have claimed that the Stone-Campbell Restoration Movement has divided more times than any other movement in history and that the Churches of Christ have divided more than any other heir of that movement. I view this from a different perspective and have come to a very different conclusion. My bachelor of arts degree at the University of Houston was in social psychology, and I did the course work equivalent of the master of arts degree in social psychology. When I came to Harding University in 1990, I taught the social psychology course for a few years. Although my master's and doctorate degrees were both in speech communication, my master's thesis was a social movement study focusing on why the Stone-Campbell Restoration Movement divided on some issues but managed to differ without dividing on other issues.[5] In my doctoral program at the University of Illinois, my cognate courses were all in psychology. In these courses I learned that people tend to notice similarities among individuals in groups with which they are less familiar, but they notice differences among individuals in their own group.[6] It is not unusual, therefore, that members of the Churches of Christ would tend to notice divisions within the Restoration Movement and especially within Churches of Christ while seeing other religious groups as being more united than they really are.

When most people hear the word "Baptist," they think of the largest Protestant denomination in America – congregations affiliated with the Southern Baptist Convention. But those who are familiar with the Southern Baptist Convention and also familiar with the heirs of the Stone-Campbell Restoration Movement generally agree that far more theological diversity exists among Southern Baptists than among all segments of the Churches of Christ. Also, the differences between the Churches of Christ and the Christian Churches are far less than the differences within the Southern Baptist Convention. Furthermore, the Southern Baptist Convention is just one of more than 30 different Baptist denominations.

In the 1980s, the Lutheran family of denominations saw the merger of three denominations into one. The American Lutheran Church, the Lutheran Church in America and the Association of Evangelical Lutheran Churches merged to form the Evangelical Lutheran Church in America. But even after that merger, there were still 13 separate Lutheran denominations in the United States.

Also in the 1980s, the Presbyterian family of denominations saw some major mergers. The Presbyterian Church in the USA and the United Presbyterian Church in the USA merged to form the Presbyterian Church (USA). Additionally, the Reformed Presbyterian Church Evangelical Synod merged into the Presbyterian Church in America. But even after those two mergers, six different Presbyterian denominations remained.

In the same way, there are 11 different Methodist denominations and 11 Mennonite denominations. Even such a small denominational family as the Friends (heirs of the Quakers) includes seven separate denominations. The list could go on and on, but this should be enough to establish the point. I am not defending division. I just want to set the current situation into the proper historical context.

## Sect, Denomination or Neither?

To understand Churches of Christ, one needs to know that Stone, Campbell and the other pioneers of the Restoration Movement believed that the church in the New Testament was neither Catholic nor Protestant. It was just Christian. They led a "Back to the Bible" movement. Their goal was to be generic Christians, not brand name Christians. They often said that they did not claim to be the only Christians, but they were trying to be Christians only. Church historians and sociologists have sometimes found that Churches of Christ and similar fellowships do not fit very well into the categories they normally use. According to some authors, a Christian religious group needs to fit into one of three categories: (1) state-established church; (2) denomination; or (3) sect. In the United States, the First Amendment to the Constitution prohibits a state-established church so that seems to leave only two categories. A Christian religious group in America today, according to these writers, must be either a sect or a denomination. But those categories did not fit what the pioneers of this movement were trying to achieve. They were trying to restore New Testament Christianity which they saw as being both non-sectarian and non-denominational.

The Bible does not discuss the sect-denomination distinction. It does not provide a good definition of the term "denomination." Most of the time when people use the word "denomination," they are talking about a group of Christians who are similar enough to one another that they see themselves as a group and that group can be identified by a name. In other words, it can be denominated. If that is all people mean by "denomination," there is no point in arguing that "Churches of Christ are not a denomination." But when sociologists and church historians talk about "sects" and "denominations," the terms have more precise meanings.

Many have used a "sect-to-denomination" framework to discuss the history of various religious groups. Richard Niebuhr's history of the Methodist Church, *The Social Sources of Denominationalism,* followed that format as have many others.[7] Most who have used this format have noted two distinctions between sect and denomination: attitudes toward other believers and attitudes toward the dominant culture. A member of a sect would insist that "The only true Christians are those who agree with me on all issues I define as being important." Sects judge all other believers to be lost. Denominations, on the other hand, judge other believers to be saved in spite of what they might see as serious errors in what those other believers teach and practice. Sects withdraw from the dominant culture while denominations have made their peace with that culture.

The main problem that I see with this sect-to-denomination model is that it treats these distinguishing characteristics as dichotomies with no possible middle ground. Personally, I strongly believe that Christians should leave it up to God to pronounce judgment concerning those who are saved and those who are lost. Doing this avoids both the sectarian and the denominational extremes. On the matter about attitudes toward the dominant culture, I believe that constructive engagement is a middle ground that is both non-sectarian and non-denominational. Christians can be "in the world" without being "of the world" (John 17:6-19).

Two other defining characteristics of denominations should be considered. One is organizational, and the other is theological. In regard to organization, a denomination is a religious group that has some level of organization above that of the local churches – some kind of central headquarters with some degree of authority over affiliated congregations. In this sense of the term, individuals do not really join a denomination. They join a local congregation that may or may not be affiliated with a denominational structure. But it is possible for a religious group to exist and function as an informal fellowship of independent congregations.

The other defining characteristic of a denomination is theological. Ecclesiology is the branch of theology dealing with doctrine concerning the church. A denominational ecclesiology affirms that denominations are a part of God's plan for the church. A nondenominational ecclesiology regards denominations as human innovations that never were a part of God's plan for the church.

Among the heirs of the Stone-Campbell Restoration Movement, the two larger groups, Churches of Christ (a cappella) and the Christian Churches and Churches of Christ (instrumental), simply do not fit the definitions of sect or denomination.

## Conclusion

Before telling the stories of people who left Churches of Christ, this background was given to show something about the fellowship they left. There are two more chapters before we get to those stories. Chapter 2 tells something of my personal story in studying patterns of growth and decline among all religious groups in America with the focus primarily on Churches of Christ. That chapter reports some important results of recent research results that have not previously been published. It also tells something of what led up to the "Why I Left Churches of Christ" survey.

Having carefully studied all of the open-ended online essays written by Christians who left Churches of Christ, I have a very strong impression that many of them would not have left if they could just have engaged in an authentic dialogue concerning the things that troubled them. I wish that I could engage in such a conversation with them even now. That, of course, is impossible because these surveys were totally anonymous. I promised to protect their privacy. When I let them tell their stories, often in their words, I may have to omit details that could reveal their identity. I may combine details from two or more stories. But in Chapter 3, I tell how I would respond if I were having a face-to-face conversation with these individuals. To do that, I need to tell what I believe about the meaning of an authentic dialogue.

Chapter 2

# Studying Patterns of Growth and Decline

Students in preaching classes often need to be reminded, "Text without context is pretext." The same thing is true when studying patterns of growth and decline in the Churches of Christ throughout the United States. Those patterns need to be considered within the context of what is happening among all religious groups in the United States. This is especially true in regard to what happens when young people grow up and leave home. Sociologists have known for a long time that early adulthood is a time in life when there is typically a decline in church membership, church attendance and other indicators of religiosity. The opening paragraph of a 2007 article on this subject is worth considering.

> The young adult years of many Americans are marked by a clear decline in outward religious expression, which is popularly thought to hit bottom during – and perhaps because of – the college experience. This is not new news. In the early 1980s, nearly 60 percent of young adults reported attending church less frequently than they did during adolescence. Dropping out of organized religion altogether is also evident.

> Estimates of religious disaffiliation in emerging adulthood typically fall between 30 and 40 percent. Seemingly no religious group is immune to this phenomenon: Catholics, Presbyterians and Mormons all lose more members during this stage of life than during any other.[1]

Most leaders in Churches of Christ regard any loss of the younger generation as being too high. But some think that this is happening for the first time with the present generation of young adults and that it is happening only in the Churches of Christ. They take this loss as evidence that something is seriously wrong with Churches of Christ. When some of those who are leaving are our children or grandchildren, it is small comfort to know that this phenomenon is not new or limited to Churches of Christ. But such knowledge might help to keep church leaders from making the wrong changes.

## Changing Climate of Receptivity Reflected by Declining Growth Rates of the Fastest-Growing Religious Groups in America

Virtually all American religious groups grew in 1945 until 1965, the two decades following the end of World War II. Since then, however, a change has taken place in the religious climate of the nation. One way to see this change is to compare the growth rates of the fastest-growing major denominations in the last three decades of the 20th century. This can be done with data from three recent decadal studies.[2] Table 2.1 shows the denominations that had the highest growth rates in three recent decades: 1970s, 1980s and 1990s. Notice how much those growth rates have declined.

In the 1970s, the Assemblies of God had the highest decadal growth rate: 70 percent. In the 1980s, the Assemblies of God were still the fastest-growing major denomination in America, but their growth rate was only 35 percent – just half of their decadal growth rate in the 1970s. In the 1990s, it was the Church of Jesus Christ of Latter-day Saints (the Mormons) who had the highest decadal growth rate: 19.3 percent. Christian Churches and Churches of Christ were close with a decadal growth rate of 18.6 percent. The Assemblies of God were also very close with a decadal growth rate of 18.5 percent. But this decline from 70 percent to 35 percent and then to only 19 percent indicates a significant change in American culture.

## Table 2.1

A Comparison of Growth Rates

| Decade | Fastest-Growing Denomination | Growth Rate |
|---|---|---|
| 1970s | Assemblies of God | 70% |
| 1980s | Assemblies of God | 35% |
| 1990s | Church of Jesus Christ of Latter-day Saints (Mormons) | 19% |

Comparisons of growth rates are considered valid only within size categories. The comparison here is limited to the 14 American religious groups with 1 million or more adherents each.[3] In the 2000 study, more than 90 percent of the adherents claimed by Christian religious bodies in America belonged to one of these fellowships. This kind of comparison is an indication of a culture's receptivity to the gospel. Donald McGavran, the father of the modern Church Growth Movement, suggested that churches should "occupy resistant fields lightly" and use more resources in places where people are more receptive.[4] He was not suggesting that Christians give up on areas such as the United States, Canada and Western Europe where people today are less receptive to the Christian message. But studying the receptivity of a culture tells where evangelism needs to start.

In 1950, when I started preaching, we could assume that most of the people around us already believed in God, in Jesus Christ as the Son of God and in the Bible as the Word of God. They already understood that people are lost in sin and in need of salvation. We could start with such people by using proof-text reasoning focused on the plan of salvation. Emphasizing the plan of salvation rather than the Savior probably produced a great number of converts who quickly dropped out of the church, but today it does not even produce many converts. The religious climate has changed.

In the 2000 study conducted by the Association of Statisticians of American Religious Bodies (ASARB), fewer than half the people in the United States were claimed as adherents by any local congregation of any of the Christian groups listed. That study was based on reports from the headquarters of denominations and reports by researchers studying groups of independent congregations. The same pattern of decline, however, was reported in a major study done with interviews of a very large random sample of individuals. According to the *U.S. Religious Landscape Survey 2008* conducted by the Pew Forum on Religion and Public Life, "More than one-quarter of American adults (28%) have left the faith in which they were raised in favor of another religion – or no religion at all." [5] Also significant was the fact that "the number of people who say that they are unaffiliated with any particular faith today (16.1%) is more than double the number who said that 20 years earlier. Among Americans ages 18-29, one-in-four say that they are not currently affiliated with any particular religion." [6] This trend is clearly reflected in Table 2.2 that ranks the largest Christian religious groups in America by their rate of growth or decline in the last decade of the 20th century.

## Table 2.2

American Religious Groups With
1 Million or More Adherents
Ranked by Rate of Growth, 1990-2000

| Religious Groups | Amount of Growth or Decline | Growth Rate |
|---|---|---|
| Church of Jesus Christ of Latter-day Saints (Mormons) | 683,206 | 19.3% |
| Christian Churches and Churches of Christ | 226,065 | 18.6% |
| Assemblies of God | 400,388 | 18.5% |
| Catholic Church | 8,649,044 | 16.2% |
| Southern Baptist Convention | 940,785 | 5.0% |
| Churches of Christ* | 43,772 | 2.7% |
| Christian Church (Disciples of Christ) | -19,973 | -2.0% |
| Evangelical Lutheran Church in America | -113,380 | -2.2% |
| Lutheran Church (Missouri Synod) | -82,663 | -3.2% |
| Episcopal Church | -130,530 | -5.3% |
| American Baptist USA | -106,269 | -6.0% |
| United Methodist Church | -740,403 | -6.7% |
| Presbyterian Church (USA) | -411,769 | -11.6% |
| United Church of Christ | -294,577 | -14.8% |

**Adjusted to account for the Crossroads/Boston Discipling Movement that in 1990 was counted with other Churches of Christ. In 1994, however, Kip McKean, who claimed apostolic authority as the leader of this movement, decided that he no longer wanted the congregations in this movement to be counted with other Churches of Christ. In 2000, they were listed as the "International Churches of Christ." At that time they had 99 congregations in the United States with 56,952 members and 79,161 adherents.*

## Recent Trends in Churches of Christ

Churches of Christ were generally regarded as being one of the fastest-growing religious groups in the United States between 1945 and 1965. But toward the end of the 1960s, several well-informed observers began to detect what they regarded as a decline in the rate of growth. Churches of Christ were still growing in number. What seemed to be declining was the rate of increase. Back then, I was preaching for a congregation that had more than 500 members and was still growing. But I saw that many other congregations were not growing as fast as they had earlier. Some had stopped growing. A few were declining. What troubled me most was that leaders in Churches of Christ had no way of knowing for sure whether this fellowship throughout the nation was growing or declining. Most denominations have research departments at denominational headquarters that study such things and regularly publish reports. Churches of Christ, however, exist and function as an informal fellowship of independent congregations with no central organizational headquarters. In a fellowship such as this, the only way for research to be done is for people to do it themselves. I decided to do that kind of research; but first I had to learn a great deal more about survey methodology and statistical analysis.

When I started studying patterns of growth and decline among Churches of Christ throughout the United States, the directories that were available were not very reliable. They were generally put together from mailing lists at a time when it was less expensive to send duplicate mailings than it was to remove duplicate listings. At one congregation where I preached, we received mailings sent to us at four different addresses. Those directories gave an inflated view regarding the number of congregations, members and adherents. But that was all that we had to work with. So I took a random sample of congregations listed and contacted them with questions about their rate of growth. That did not tell how many congregations, members or adherents Churches of Christ had throughout the nation, but it at least gave some estimates of growth rates.

For several years, I continued sampling congregations to estimate the nationwide rate of growth in Churches of Christ. Such surveys were no longer needed after the directories became more accurate. Mac Lynn spent many years conducting nationwide census studies of congregations.[7] His work was, by far, the greatest contribution that has ever been made to this kind of research among Churches of Christ in the United States. When the leaders of the Association of Statisticians of American Religious Bodies (ASARB) learned about the church census work Lynn was doing among Churches of Christ, they invited him to become a member. Eventually he became the president of ASARB and was one of the compilers of the almanac *Churches and Church Membership in the United States 1990*. I became a member of ASARB because of my survey research among Churches of Christ. Carl Royster, the current compiler of the directory, *Churches of Christ in the United States* is also a member of this organization of church statisticians.

I tried to continue my ministry as a preacher in full-time local church work and combine that with my interest in church-growth research, writing and consulting. That did not work out very well. I found it much easier to fulfill those interests when combined with a career in higher education. I took a position as chairman of the speech communication program at the University of Tulsa. That is where I was when I started writing articles for religious journals reporting a decline in the growth rate among Churches of Christ in the United States. The nationwide research indicated that if the 1965 through 1975 trend continued, Churches of Christ would reach zero level growth by 1980. When I reported this information, some people started calling me the "Brotherhood Prophet of Gloom and Doom." But it actually happened! In 1980, nationwide figures on Churches of Christ reached zero level growth. Since 1980, the growth "curves" for the numbers of congregations, members, adherents and attendance have been essentially flat. "Plateaued" is a term that church statisticians use to describe the condition in which a religious group does not grow significantly or decline significantly. That is what happened in Churches of Christ from 1980 until a high point of sorts was reached in 2003. In the period from 1980 to 2003, the average annual rate of change was never greater than one half of 1 percent, plus or minus. These year-to-year changes were very small. But between 2003 and 2009, Churches of Christ in the United States declined by 4.0 percent in the number of congregations, 4.1 percent in the number of members and 4.7 percent in the number of adherents.[8] That decline is large enough and has gone on long enough to be significant.

## A Different Kind of Outcomes Assessment Research

After moving to Harding University in 1990, I served as director of the Office of Outcomes Assessment along with my teaching duties in the College of Bible and Religion and my work as the Director of the Harding Center for Church Growth Studies. The Office of Outcomes Assessment is responsible for doing the kind of survey research and statistical analysis needed for periodic reviews by accrediting agencies. In 1994 and 2004, Harding University had successful reviews by the Higher Learning Commission of North Central Association of Colleges and Schools. After the 2004 review, I retired from the Outcomes Assessment position and returned to full-time teaching and research in the College of Bible and Religion. That is what I continued doing until I retired at the end of the spring semester in 2011. After that, I have continued doing research and writing.

In 2005, Dr. David B. Burks, president of Harding University, told me that for several years the presidents of Christian colleges and universities had been discussing the need for some collective research on outcomes of Christian higher education. He asked me to prepare a proposal for research that would provide reliable and recent answers to some questions of special interest to the presidents of Christian colleges and universities. These questions also included some that were of interest to all church leaders. I prepared the research proposal. The presidents of Christian colleges and universities considered it in the meeting of the Christian Higher Education Foundation. They approved my proposal, and I started collecting data.

## Research Questions

1. Questions of special interest to the presidents of Christian colleges and universities:
   - How many young people in Churches of Christ graduate from high school in the United States each year?
   - How many of these high school graduates go on to attend college?
   - How many of these college-bound young people attend a Christian college or university?
   - What difference does attending a Christian college or university make?
   - Are those who attend a Christian college or university more likely to stay in the Churches of Christ later in life?
   - Are the alumni of these schools more likely to have leadership or service roles in the church?
   - Is the divorce rate among the graduates of these schools lower than the national average?
2. Questions of general interest to all church leaders:
   - How many of the recent high school graduates in Churches of Christ now have any kind of leadership or service roles indicating involvement with a local congregation?
   - What is the divorce rate among recent high school graduates in Churches of Christ?
   - How many young people in Churches of Christ leave this fellowship after they graduate from high school and leave home?
   - How many of these join some other religious group?
   - How many have no present religious affiliation?
   - What factors influenced retention rates in Churches of Christ?

## Research Methods

- More than 2,000 students at 11 Christian colleges and universities participated in a student survey.
- More than 2,500 alumni of these same schools participated in an alumni survey.
- Eighty leaders of campus ministries conducted by Churches of Christ at state-supported colleges and universities provided data on these ministries, and 404 students involved in campus ministry activities responded to a survey.

- In a cluster sampling of 100 congregations, church leaders provided data on 4,993 young people in their congregations who had graduated from high school in the previous 10 years, 1997-2006.

Previous research had found that those who have left Churches of Christ do not generally respond to our surveys. What was used here, therefore, was an indirect approach. The first step was to select 100 congregations that matched norms for Churches of Christ in the United States in regard to location, church size and the racial/ethnic character of the congregation. This was done by sending a research packet to more than 5,000 Churches of Christ throughout the nation. The instructions for each congregation asked church leaders to make a list of all the members of their congregation who had graduated from high school in 1997 through 2006. Then those church leaders were asked a few relatively simple questions about each person.

- Is this person still a member of your congregation or of another congregation of the Churches of Christ?
- If so, do they have any leadership or service roles in the church?
- If not, have they joined some other religious group?
- If they have joined some other religious group, which group did they join?
- What is their marital status?
- Did they attend college?
- If so, did they attend a Christian college or university?
- If they attended another kind of school, did they become actively involved with a local congregation while they were in school – and with a campus ministry if Churches of Christ had such a ministry at that school?

The church leaders who filled out this form often had to obtain the help of youth ministers, high school Bible class teachers, parents, grandparents or friends. I knew, however, that it is possible to collect accurate data in this way. In the past 40 years, I have conducted more than 100 congregational assessments that used this indirect method of collecting data.

## Some of the Results

- One percent of the adherents in the 100 congregations of the cluster sample graduated from high school each year. That is exactly the same as the percentage in the U.S. population generally.

- Among the 4,993 young Christians who graduated from high school while attending these 100 congregations of the cluster sample, 80.2 percent went on to attend college. That is well above the national average of just a little less than two-thirds of high school graduates going on to attend college.
- Among the college-bound recent high school graduates in the 100 congregations of the cluster sample, 37.5 percent attended a Christian college or university. That is far higher than the estimate of 15 percent we have often heard in recent years.

Before going further with the presentation of results, we need to consider the validity of this cluster sampling. If this cluster sample accurately represents Churches of Christ through the nation, we should be able to use the three percentages listed above to estimate the number of members of the Churches of Christ among the entering freshmen at Christian colleges and universities. A great majority of young people from Churches of Christ who enroll at a Christian college or university come from what the directory *Churches of Christ in the United States* lists as "mainstream" congregations. So I took 1.0 percent of the total number of adherents in "mainstream" Churches of Christ as the estimate of those graduating from high school. Then I took 80.2 percent of that number as the estimate of those who were college-bound. Finally, I took 37.5 percent of that figure as the estimate of how many high school graduates from Churches of Christ would enroll as freshmen at one of the Christian colleges or universities serving this church constituency.

The next step was to contact these schools and ask how many members of the Churches of Christ enrolled as freshmen in each year of this study, 1997 through 2006. Those reports came from 15 Christian colleges and universities in the United States and two small schools in Canada.

Abilene Christian University, Abilene, Texas
Crowley's Ridge College, Paragould, Ark.
Faulkner University, Montgomery, Ala.
Freed-Hardeman University, Henderson, Tenn.
Great Lakes Christian College, Beamsville, Ontario, Canada
Harding University, Searcy, Ark.
Heritage Christian University, Florence, Ala.

Lipscomb University, Nashville, Tenn.
Lubbock Christian University, Lubbock, Texas
Magnolia Bible College, Kosciusko, Miss.
Ohio Valley University, Vienna, W.Va.
Oklahoma Christian University, Oklahoma City, Okla.
Pepperdine University, Malibu, Calif.
Rochester College, Rochester Hills, Mich.
Southwestern Christian College, Terrell, Texas
Western Christian College, Regina, Saskatchewan, Canada
York College, York, Neb.

Table 2.3 shows the results of this comparison:

## Table 2.3

Comparing Estimated and Reported Freshmen Enrollment at Christian Colleges and Universities of Students Who Are Members of the Churches of Christ

| Year | Estimated Number | Reported Number | Difference |
|---|---|---|---|
| 1997 | 4,309 | 3,664 | 645 |
| 1998 | 4,307 | 3,757 | 550 |
| 1999 | 4,306 | 4,351 | -45 |
| 2000 | 4,305 | 4,411 | -106 |
| 2001 | 4,325 | 4,461 | -146 |
| 2002 | 4,326 | 4,060 | 266 |
| 2003 | 4,335 | 4,034 | 301 |
| 2004 | 4,321 | 4,209 | 112 |
| 2005 | 4,307 | 4,175 | 132 |
| 2006 | 4,293 | 4,029 | 264 |
| **Totals** | 43,124 | 41,151 | 1,973 |
| **Averages** | 4,321 | 4,115 | 206 |

This estimate was off by less than 5.0 percent. That is strong evidence that the cluster sample of 100 congregations accurately represented Churches of Christ throughout the nation. For future planning purposes, the estimate would be closer if the number of college-bound high school graduates in Churches of Christ who attend a Christian college or university is figured at 35.5 percent.

The following are some other results found in this study – beginning with some indications of marital stability as reflected in divorce statistics.

- Among more than 2,500 alumni of 11 Christian colleges and universities, 6.9 percent of those who had ever married had eventually divorced. But a divorce rate of less than 7.0 percent is far lower than the national average.
- Among the 4,993 Christian young people who graduated from high school in one of the 100 congregations of the cluster sample, most had not yet married. But among those who had married, only 4.2 percent had divorced. The divorce rate was 8.1 percent for this same age group cohort according to U.S. Census Bureau figures.
- Note, however, that most members of the Churches of Christ are not alumni of a Christian college or university, and most did not graduate from high school between 1997 and 2006. If we knew the marital status of all members of the Churches of Christ in the United States, the divorce rate would probably be much higher. An "educated guess" is that it probably would be around 25 to 30 percent.

Some may have trouble believing this report about divorce rates in Churches of Christ because they have so often heard the claim that "[t]he divorce rate in the United States is highest in the South where conservative, evangelical and fundamentalist denominations claim the greatest number of adherents." It is true that the highest divorce rate in the United States is in the South.[9] It is also true that the South is where the congregations affiliated with the Southern Baptist Convention and several other conservative religious groups have the largest number of adherents.[10] What this claim overlooks is that the Southern Baptist Convention and most other conservative, evangelical denominations report average attendance figures less than half the number they claim as adherents – as reported in Chapter 1, Table 1.2.[11]

What this means is that many of the people classified as conservative, evangelical, fundamentalist or "born again" Christians have only a marginal connection with the church. In Churches of Christ, the average attendance figure is 76.4 percent of the reported number of adherents. If the adherent figure for Churches of Christ were inflated to include all the former members who have not attended church services anywhere for years, the divorce rate would probably be closer to the national average.

## Retention Rates in Churches of Christ

In the early 1990s, there was some nationwide research conducted by Lewis, Dodd and Tippens that included an estimate of retention rates in Churches of Christ.[12] Their estimate was that only 55 percent of the young people growing up in Churches of Christ maintain that church affiliation after they grow up and leave home. That leaves 45 percent who do not. That 55 percent figure is exactly what I found in more than 100 congregational assessments, but I found something different about the rest. I found that around 33 percent leave Churches of Christ as soon as they grow up and leave home, and they never come back to Churches of Christ. But the remaining 12 percent stop attending Churches of Christ when they leave home but then return to Churches of Christ after they mature, get married and start having children. Those, however, are not recent estimates.

Among the 4,993 young people in the 100 congregations of the cluster sample used in this study – those who graduated from high school between 1997 and 2006:

- 58.2 percent are still members of some local congregation of the Churches of Christ;
- 21.1 percent have joined some other religious group; and,
- 20.7 percent have no present religious affiliation.

Among more than 2,500 alumni of 11 Christian colleges and universities, 85.1 percent are still members of the Churches of Christ.

These, of course, are just two "snapshots" and not the whole picture. The alumni surveys were distributed by the Office of Alumni Relations at each of the 11 participating schools, and that may have biased the results. Alumni who had not divorced and who were still members of the Churches of Christ may have been more likely to respond. I have seen some survey results conducted at websites that appear to be visited more by people who have left Churches of Christ and people who have divorced. Those surveys may be biased in the opposite direction. Reality is probably somewhere in between.

The focus of this book is on improving the retention rate. The goal of this study is to help church leaders learn what they can do to reduce the number who leave.

## Three Factors That Influence Retention Rates

Many factors influence retention rates. For example, I did a survey that was reported in a *Youth Ministry Bulletin* in 1985.[13] That study identified three factors that were associated with a higher-than-average retention rate among young people growing up in congregations of the Churches of Christ.

1. The presence of an active youth ministry. Congregations did not need to have a full-time church-supported youth ministry, but they at least needed an active youth ministry with special programs and activities for the young people.
2. A challenging curriculum in adult Bible classes. I thought that we would find a difference in the classes for young people. There was, however, so much variation in the sample that the differences were not statistically significant. At the adult level, however, the difference was statistically significant. Some church leaders seem to assume that the adults will put up with anything to get their children into good Bible classes. In these churches, adult members are never challenged to learn anything new. They just rehearse the doctrine week after week. But in these churches, the members do not attend the watered-down adult Bible classes and do not bring their children. Furthermore, adults in these congregations are not taught how to bring up their children "in the nurture and admonition of the Lord" (Ephesians 6:4 KJV).
3. The level of parental attendance and involvement in the church. When the average parents in the congregation attend regularly and have specific church work assignments, their children are much more likely to remain in Churches of Christ after they grow up and leave home. The retention rate in those churches was around 75 to 80 percent. In congregations where the average family has one parent who is an active and involved member but the other is not, the retention rate was around 50 percent. In churches where the typical family was one in which neither parent was active and involved, the retention rate was around 20 to 25 percent.

These are probably still significant factors. But another study conducted for the Christian Higher Education Foundation asked different questions and found three other factors discussed in the following sections.

## The Character of the Congregation Where Young People Grew Up

One of the questions church leaders were asked in this study was, "How do you think other members of the Churches of Christ would regard your congregation?" There were five response options:

- Much more liberal or progressive;
- A little more liberal or progressive;
- Middle-of-the-road, moderate;
- A little more conservative or traditional; and
- Much more conservative or traditional.

These terms, of course, are very subjective. No definitions were given. The answers to this question, therefore, called for these church leaders to report their perception of how other members of the Churches of Christ would perceive them. That is at least two or three steps away from reality. But there must be some common understanding because the results were not random. Table 2.4 shows the five church character categories, with the number of congregations in each category, the number of recent high school graduates in each group of congregations and the retentions of these young people.

## Table 2.4

The Influence of Congregational Character on Retention Rates

| Congregational Character | No. of Churches | No. of Recent H.S. Grads | Retention Rate |
|---|---|---|---|
| Much more liberal or progressive | 8 | 374 | 39.4% |
| A little more liberal or progressive | 15 | 759 | 55.2% |
| Middle-of-the-road, moderate | 53 | 2,706 | 62.0% |
| A little more conservative or traditional | 16 | 804 | 58.0% |
| Much more conservative or traditional | 8 | 350 | 39.9% |
| TOTALS and Average | 100 | 4,993 | 57.9% |

The lowest retention rates were in the congregations that differed the most from the middle-of-the-road or moderate congregations – if the perceptions of church leaders regarding the perceptions of others were accurate. That, of course, is just what, not why. Here is a possible explanation. When they leave home, young people who grew up in a congregation that is much more liberal or much more conservative than most other congregations, might find it difficult to find a church like their home church.

Please note that this is not an argument in favor of doing theology by opinion polls. Christians must stay with what they honestly believe to be the truth of God's Word, no matter how unpopular it might be. But just from a sociological or historical perspective, these results are worth considering. Furthermore, they may simply illustrate the danger of extremism. But the problem is not just liberal extremism or conservative extremism. The problem is extremism. God's instructions to Joshua might be good for Christians today to remember: "Only be strong and very courageous, being careful to do according to all the law that Moses my servant commanded you. Do not turn from it to the right hand or to the left, that you may have good success wherever you go" (Joshua 1:7). I believe that we could borrow that language and apply the principle in Churches of Christ today. In actual practice, someone is regarded as being "too liberal" if his conscience permits something that my conscience does not permit. Likewise, a person is "too conservative" if his conscience forbids something that I think is acceptable. This, of course, is a very self-centered definition; but in practice that is how the terms are used.

No statistically significant difference was observed between the retention rates of the "liberal" and "conservative" churches. However, the differences between these churches and those in the middle were significant. One other statistically significant difference was based on congregational character. That difference was in regard to where the drop-outs went when they left Churches of Christ.

## Table 2.5

Influence of Congregational Character on Where the Drop-Outs Go

| Congregational Character | Joined Another Religious Group | No Present Religious Affiliation |
|---|---|---|
| Much more liberal or progressive | 75.2% | 24.5% |
| A little more liberal or progressive | 66.6% | 33.4% |

| | | |
|---|---|---|
| Middle-of-the-road, moderate | 47.2% | 52.2% |
| A little more conservative or traditional | 32.1% | 67.9% |
| Much more conservative or traditional | 24.8% | 75.2% |

As shown in Table 2.5, three-fourths of the drop-outs from the most liberal congregations joined some other religious group when they left home and left the Churches of Christ. Among those from the most conservative churches only one-fourth joined another religious group, but a large percentage had no religious affiliation. The same pattern of joining another religious group is seen when the two more liberal groups are averaged and compared with the average of the two more conservative groups.

## Decisions about College Education

One of the things related to the number of people who stayed in Churches of Christ was the decision they made about college, as shown in Table 2.6. The lowest retention rate was among those who decided not to attend college. The highest retention rate was among those who attended a Christian college or university. The third category, however, calls for some clarification. Among the young people from Churches of Christ who attend some school other than a Christian college or university, 85 percent stop attending church services as soon as they leave home.[14] However, that is not the end of the story. After they graduate, get married and have children, more than one-third start attending church services once again. So the ultimate retention rate among those who attend anything other than a Christian college or university is 49.7 percent.[15]

## Table 2.6

Decisions Regarding College as a Factor in Retention Rate Among Members of the Churches of Christ

| Decision About College | Retention Rates |
|---|---|
| 19.8% did not attend college | 43.4% |
| 31.4% attended a Christian college or university | 85.0% |
| 48.8% attended a public college or university | 49.7% |

More than half of those who drop out of Churches of Christ when they enroll at a state-supported college or university never come back. Those who come back do so without the Bible knowledge and leadership training that others received at a Christian college or university. In my opinion, retention in Churches of Christ is not as strong an argument in favor of Christian higher education as is preparation for church leadership.

## Church Attendance and Involvement

Alumni who attended a Christian college or university and also became actively involved as members of a local congregation while they were in school had the highest retention rate observed in this study. It is important to note, however, that the second-highest retention rate was among those Christian young people who attended some other kind of school but also became actively involved as members of a local congregation while they were in school. If Churches of Christ had a campus ministry at that school, these students became active participants. Actually the difference between these two groups, while in the direction of favoring those attending Christian colleges or universities, was not statistically significant.

In my personal opinion, those of us who believe in the value of Christian higher education should not try to promote Christian colleges or universities by attacking public higher education. Instead, we should recognize that campus ministries are partners in Christian higher education. We should support the few campus ministries that Churches of Christ already operate, and we should establish many more.

The surveys of 100 congregations in the cluster sample provided some information on the levels of attendance and involvement among almost 5,000 young people from their congregations. Some of the data on the present practices of students came from surveys of more than 2,000 students at 11 Christian colleges and universities. These were compared with what more than 2,500 alumni said their practices had been when they were in school. The alumni were asked how often they had attended church services and what their level of involvement was in a local congregation when they were in school.

For purposes of this study, participants were asked to select the statement that came closest to describing their level of church involvement.

- Members. "My home congregation was close enough so that I was still a member and continued to attend services at my home congregation" or "After I enrolled at this school, I placed membership with a local congregation where I attend services."

- **Regular Visitors.** "Although I never actually placed membership, there was a local congregation where I attended services most of the time."
- **Floaters.** "Although I attended services regularly, I visited several different congregations depending on where my friends were going and what special classes or speakers were scheduled."
- **Occasional Visitors.** "I occasionally visited various congregations, but I did not attend church services regularly anywhere."
- **Non-Attenders.** "I did not attend church services at any congregation."

As Table 2.7 shows, what alumni did about church involvement while they were in school was related to retention rates in Churches of Christ. When students are merely occasional visitors while in school, the tendency is for them to remain as spectators later in life. Many of these eventually drop out of Churches of Christ.

## Table 2.7

Levels of Involvement in Church While in School as a Factor in Retention Rates

| Levels | Retention Rates |
|---|---|
| "Members" | 96.9% |
| "Regular Visitors" | 81.9% |
| "Floaters" | 68.2% |
| "Occasional Visitors" | 12.0% |
| "Non-Attenders" | 0.0% |

Given the importance of students being involved in local churches while attending a Christian college or university, the data reported in Table 2.8 are cause for serious concern. In the 11 Christian colleges and universities involved in this study, only one-fourth of the students are actually involved as members of a local congregation. Fewer than one-third of the alumni reported that they were involved as members of a local congregation when they were in school. But both of these figures are far too low.

## Table 2.8

Levels of Involvement in Local Churches by Students and Alumni at 11 Christian Colleges and Universities

| Levels | Students | Alumni |
| --- | --- | --- |
| "Members" | 25.2% | 31.2% |
| "Regular Visitors" | 52.5% | 39.8% |
| "Floaters" | 15.0% | 27.4% |
| "Occasional Visitors" | 6.5% | 2.6% |
| "Non-Attenders" | 1.3% | 0.3% |

When administrators at Christian colleges and universities saw these reports, many began serious efforts to persuade students to become involved members of a local congregation and attend church services regularly. At Harding University, Dr. Bruce McLarty, the vice president for spiritual life, used chapel and Bible classes to show students the importance of getting involved with a local congregation. He also met with elders and preachers from area congregations and talked to them about things congregations could do to put students to work. In the spring semester of 2009, McLarty had students in all Bible classes take a follow-up survey of church attendance and involvement. Results showed significant improvement in the past two years. But the results also showed that plenty of room remained for improvement.

This study was repeated in the spring of 2011. Results showed that among students who are members of the Churches of Christ there was a significant increase in the average number of times per month that they attended church services.

| | |
| --- | --- |
| In the 2006 study | 6.8 times per month |
| In the 2009 study | 7.6 times per month |
| In the 2011 study | 9.7 times per month |

One out of five in the most recent study said that they were actually members of a local congregation. Almost 7 percent more (6.7%) said they at least told church leaders that they wanted that congregation to be their "church home away from home" while attending Harding. Almost half (49.3%) said that there was one congregation they visited regularly without really being involved. Almost one out of five (18.6%)

said that they just visit various congregations, and 2.7 percent said that they had not attended any local congregation in the 2010-2011 academic year. So there is still room for improvement.

## Conclusion: Going on to the Next Step

The character of the congregation in which young Christians grow up, the decision they make about college and their level of involvement with another congregation after they leave home were the three factors identified in this study associated with retention rates. I reported these findings to the presidents of Christian colleges and universities in the 2008 meeting of the Christian Higher Education Foundation. I thought that this would be my final report to them. It turned out, however, that they had more research questions they wanted answered. They wanted to know more about the people who are leaving Churches of Christ, where they are going and why they are leaving. I agreed to study those issues.

The data from the cluster sample of 100 congregations had already provided some general results regarding some who are leaving Churches of Christ. The indirect approach used in that study partially overcame the problem about those who have left Churches of Christ not responding to our surveys. In that approach, church leaders provided objective answers to a few questions, but that did not give those who have left an opportunity to speak. Something else was needed.

The approach used in the present study involved setting up a website to host an online survey called "Why I Left Churches of Christ." An article in *The Christian Chronicle*, the leading newspaper read by members of the Churches of Christ, announced this survey. The presidents of Christian colleges and universities personally contacted people they knew who had left Churches of Christ and asked them to consider responding to this online survey. These presidents encouraged members of their faculties to do the same thing. Many of the church leaders in the congregations of the original cluster sample made personal contacts asking former members to participate in this study. By the time this website was taken down in July 2009, many more than 300 individuals had written essays responding to a few basic questions:

- Why did you leave Churches of Christ?
- Where did you go?

- What is your present religious affiliation?
- Are your spiritual needs being fulfilled better in the church you are now attending than they were in Churches of Christ? If so, how?
- Do you have any advice for leaders in Churches of Christ that might help them do a better job of ministering to those who have not left?

This kind of survey obviously does not produce a random sample. Whether it is representative is something that you and the other readers of this book will have to judge for yourselves on the basis of how closely these stories match the things you have observed in your congregation and other Churches of Christ. I did not teach Bible classes at Harding University in the summer of 2009. Instead, I carefully read all of the essay responses looking for patterns and themes. I had the help of others in doing content analysis. This is a departure from the kind of analysis I have usually done in survey research. But as I told the presidents, "Sometimes words are more important than numbers."

In this kind of research, it is not essential to have a very large sample. What is essential is that there are enough responses to include all of the kinds of things people are saying. By the time we passed the 200 or 250 mark in this study, the responses did not say much that was new. They just said the same things in different words. That repetition, however, was very useful. It added to the richness of the data base, and it provided more variety in the personal stories. It also helped to rank categories of responses according to how often they were mentioned.

Some church leaders see no value in this kind of research. "Why should we listen to those who have left us?" they ask. But I believe that we can learn much from those who have left. I certainly am not the first to do this kind of study. In 1993, William D. Hendricks wrote *Exit Interviews: Revealing Stories of Why People Are Leaving the Church.*[16] In the business world and in academia, such exit interviews are common assessment tools. If the only people church leaders listen to are those who give them praise, they may not be hearing the most important things they need to hear. Those who are leaving a congregation are voting with their feet, and their vote is one of "no confidence." By their leaving, they are telling church leaders that something is wrong. The fault may be with those who leave. Some may be like those John wrote about in 1 John 2:19, "They went out from us, but they were not of us; for if they had been of us, they would have continued with us. But they went out, that it might become plain that they all are not of us."[17] When you read their stories in Part 2 of this book, you will likely see some examples that fit this pattern. But I believe that you will see many others that do not.

Frankly, I have found it extremely difficult to read these stories. A few of these people are very angry, and often I can understand their anger. Far more of the stories are about people who have been hurt and neglected. As I read their stories, I identified with them and honestly felt their pain. I also felt grief for the failure of Christians in general and church leaders in particular to care enough to reach out to these people before they left or to seek them after they left in an effort to bring them back.

The format that I have followed in Part 2 is to use categories of similar stories. As much as possible, I have tried to let these people speak in their own words – but always protecting their privacy. However, I cannot tell you their stories without my personal responses that reveal something of my story. Giving voice to those who have left Churches of Christ and adding my personal reflections may be controversial. That kind of self-disclosure involves risks. Almost everyone is likely to object to something I say. That is why I told the presidents of Christian colleges and universities that while I appreciated their encouragement, I wanted to do this study personally. I did not want this to be done under the sponsorship of the Christian Higher Education Foundation, Harding University or any other Christian college or university. The presidents of these schools have enough to do without having to deal with critics who may not like what I say in this book.

However, my hope and prayer are that the readers of these stories will learn from them so that Churches of Christ may improve the ministry to those who have not left. But before we hear their stories and respond as though engaged in an authentic dialogue, we first need to consider the nature of authentic dialogue. That is the subject of Chapter 3.

Chapter **3**

# Communicating With Those Who Left

Reading more than 300 open-ended essay responses to the "Why I Left Churches of Christ" survey left me with a very strong impression. I am convinced that many of these Christians would not have left if someone had communicated with them in the right way. I am not saying, "What we've got here is a failure to communicate," as in the famous line from the 1967 film *Cool Hand Luke*. Successful communication does not always mean that the people involved agree. Sometimes they have a fundamental clash of values, as was the case in that movie. All that I am saying is that the right kind of communication could have helped with these people who left Churches of Christ. Unfortunately, however, many people just do not recognize the importance of communication.

## The Importance of Communication

Suppose that fish had human characteristics and could speculate about the meaning of their existence and their place in the universe. My guess, even then, is that fish would probably be the last of all creatures to discover water. Because water is such a constant part of their environment, fish would probably take it for granted. That fish story illustrates something important about people. We live in a sea of communication, but that communication is such a constant part of our environment that we take it for granted.

To illustrate the importance of communication, I sometimes ask my students to use their imaginations and consider a question: What would happen if you could produce a living human body in total isolation from all other humans and with no human contact or human communication at all? Suppose that you started with a donor egg and sperm combined in a Petri dish in a laboratory. Suppose that you had a robot place the fertilized egg into an artificial womb. Then after nine months of fetal development, suppose that you had the robot deliver the baby and immediately place it in a life-support chamber. Suppose that in this isolation chamber all physical needs would be provided, and physical life could be sustained for many years. But suppose that this human would never experience any other human contact or communication. Then, suppose that after many years you opened that isolation chamber. What would you find?

Some of my students usually say that you would find the remains of a dead baby. Without the stimulation provided by human interaction, the baby would not survive. But I tell my students that they were supposed to use their imaginations. The conditions of this quiz stipulated that the machine would be able to sustain physical life for many years. So I ask them again to tell me what they would find after many years when they opened the imaginary isolation chamber. How would you answer that question?

I believe that one would find animal life at the level of reflex and instinct, but nothing more. The living creature in that isolation chamber would show signs of fear, anger, rage and similar animal passions; but it would show no evidence of mind or personhood, no awareness of self as distinct from others. We learn language from language users. If you had never communicated with others, you would not know any language at all. In fact, if there were no interaction with others, there would be no you.

It would clearly be unethical and immoral to conduct such an experiment. But there have been some natural experiments – events that came close to replicating such an experiment. There have been a few documented cases of feral children lost or abandoned in some forest or jungle and then cared for by wild animals. John Stewart tells about one such case in his textbook on interpersonal communication.[1] The story involved a remarkable creature that came out of the woods near a small town in Southern France. This creature was captured while digging for vegetables in a village garden. Roger Shattuck tells about this creature in his book *The Forbidden Experiment: The Story of the Wild Boy of Aveyron*. He wrote that this creature " ... was human in bodily form and walked erect. Everything else about him suggested an animal. He was naked except for the tatters of a shirt and showed no modesty, no awareness of himself as a human person related in any way to the people who captured him. He could not speak and made only weird, meaningless cries. Though very short, he appeared to be a boy of about eleven or twelve."[2] This "Savage of Aveyron" did not begin to display uniquely human characteristics until after he was cared for by a foster family. Stewart concluded "Without that contact, this human organism was a 'creature,' a 'savage,' with it he began to develop into a person."[3]

In a folk tale among the people of Northern India, there is a legend that many people claim to be factual. In this story, all of the people of a village had been killed except for a baby girl. This baby, it appears, was "adopted" by a wolf pack and nursed by a wolf. Later people reported seeing a young girl running with a pack of wolves. Eventually she was captured. She appeared to be a human female about 10 or 11 years of age, but she had no uniquely human characteristics. She walked like a wolf, growled like a wolf, ate like a wolf and smelled like a wolf. She could not speak. This "wolf girl," according to the story, was never civilized. She died after about one year of captivity.

The most dramatic story of this kind is the story of Helen Keller. When she was a very young child, she had an illness that left her both blind and deaf. She survived the illness and grew to be about the size of a normal teenager, but she was almost totally isolated. At least 98 percent of our contact with the external world comes through what we see and hear. Helen, therefore, was at least 98 percent of the way into something like the isolation chamber discussed earlier. She had no language. She could not communicate. She was, in fact, very much like a wild animal.

Finally, Helen's father arranged for Annie Sullivan to be Helen's teacher. Annie made the signs of the deaf language in Helen's hands and taught her to mimic those signs. But at first those signs had no meaning for Helen. They did not function as symbols that represented anything. If you are familiar with *The Miracle Worker* (a book, play and movie) you probably already know that Annie took Helen to a pump at a well. She made the sign for "water" while pumping water on Helen's hand. That was what Gestalt psychology calls the "Aha!" experience. It was the moment of insight. That is when Helen understood that the hand sign for water stood for the cool wet liquid that she drank. Once Helen understood that the hand signs represented things, she could learn how to communicate. Helen Keller eventually became a very intelligent person, but she was like a wild animal before she learned how to communicate.

Communication with others is what develops and sustains authentic selfhood. As you grew up, you were influenced by parents, siblings, members of your extended family, teachers, friends and anyone who played a significant role in your life. As you identified with these people, you incorporated them into your unique personhood. They became part of you. That is how you became who and what you are. Heredity sets some important limits. Environment is a powerful influence. But how you choose to react to your heredity and your environment is ultimately what makes you the unique person you become.

## The Kind of Communication That Imparts a Blessing

In their book *The Blessing*, Smalley and Trent discuss a special kind of communication that can impart a blessing in the parent-child relationship.[4] But this is not a new discovery. Two thousand years ago, Paul wrote in Ephesians 4:29: "Let no corrupting talk come out of your mouths, but only such as is good for building up, as fits the occasion, that it may give grace to those who hear." Other translations have "impart grace" (NKJV); "minister grace" (KJV); "result in spiritual blessing to the hearers" (Williams); "be a means of blessing to the hearers" (Weymouth); and "words that are gracious and a means of grace to those who hear them" (Moffatt). The various translations of this verse clearly show that a kind of communication imparts a blessing. But that insight is not limited to Christians. The Jewish existentialist philosopher Martin Buber wrote about a special kind of communication that treats people as subjects rather than objects. Treating people as objects, according to Buber, tends to be dehumanizing. The "I-Thou" kind of communication, Buber wrote, imparts a blessing that the "I-It" kind of communication cannot impart.[5]

Communication is essential in your quest to become yourself, but some kinds of communication do not help. Before we discuss the good kind of communication, it may be useful to examine some kinds of communication that are destructive. Some forms of communication may pressure you to become an inferior imitation of someone else. One of my favorite Martin Buber stories is about a rabbi who tried all his life to become another Moses without success. Finally he died and stood before God in judgment. And God said, "You are not condemned for your failure to become another Moses. Another Moses I did not need. A Moses I already had. You are condemned for your failure to become yourself." Some churches have gone from being authoritarian to being totalitarian. They insist on having absolute control in the lives of their members. These churches practice a kind of cult-like mind control without really intending to do so. The group dynamics in these churches produces a cloning effect. Members are pressured to conform in ways that have nothing to do with Christianity. Christians, of course, are supposed to change and be made over after the image of God as His nature is revealed in the person of Jesus Christ (Ephesians 4:21-24). But pressure to conform in ways that have nothing to do with Christianity can damage people psychologically and spiritually.[6]

I have observed a strange pattern when counseling alcoholics and their families. I would often see a battered wife who was abused physically and verbally by an alcoholic husband. Eventually she would take my advice and escape from that abusive relationship. But the strange thing that happened all too often was that such a woman would soon marry another alcoholic wife beater. Of course it did not always happen that way. The wonder is that it ever happened. How could a woman who had endured that kind of hell on earth ever get back into that situation? Some of these women had learned to play only one role in life: the role of victim. It is not much fun to hurt, but in some sick way it may be better than feeling nothing at all. They cannot, however, play the role of victim without someone to play the role of persecutor. The wrong kind of communication can influence people to play roles in life that are something less than the fully functioning, autonomous, unique persons they could have become.

Communication can be used to trick, deceive and manipulate. Have you ever bought something that you would not have bought if you had known then what the sales person knew? If so, you were manipulated. In Buber's language, you were treated as an object rather than as a person. The greatest immorality, in my opinion, is to love things and use people. Control is a sick way of relating to people.

Some communication treats others as mere audience, not as unique individuals. The "one size fits all" kind of message is like that. The memorized sales pitch used by telemarketers fits this category. This kind of communication is not especially damaging, but it contributes nothing to the development of authentic selfhood. If that were all that a person heard, what do you suppose he or she would become?

Have you ever engaged in a "duologue" (two monologues that go on at the same time without ever meeting)? If so, you know what it feels like to feel invisible. It is as though neither of you was really present and available to the other. In a dialogue, when you send a message to the other person, his or her response is supposed to have something to do with what you just said. In a duologue, however, the other message has nothing to do with your original message. At that point, you have to decide whether to get on the subject he or she is discussing or stick with your original subject. If you continue the duologue, you stick with your original subject and the other person sticks with his or hers. Both of you continue talking, but you are talking past each other and not with each other.

In Ephesians 4:29, Paul warned against the kind of "corrupting talk" that does not impart a blessing. Some messages are more like a curse than a blessing. Some of the counselors who use Eric Berne's system of Transactional Analysis talk about "witch messages."[7] I saw the effects of a witch message when I was counseling a young boy at a children's home in Tulsa. His mother had told him repeatedly, "You are just like your uncle who died in the electric chair, and you probably will die the same way." This young boy was well on his way toward a life of crime until the houseparents and others at the home persuaded him that he did not have to live out that witch message. He could write his own script.

Many kinds of unwholesome speech do not impart a blessing. But fortunately, there is also the good kind of speech that does impart a blessing. "Authentic dialogue" is the term many writers have used for this good kind of communication. It is called "authentic" because it authenticates. It treats the other person as a person and not as an object to be manipulated. Authentic dialogue is the kind of communication in which each person, in effect, says to the other, "Here is who I am and what I am. Here is how I see the world. Now let me learn who and what you are. Tell me how you see the world. You look at the world for a while through my eyes, and let me look at the world through your eyes."

The goal in such a dialogue is to understand and be understood. Each participant in a dialogue may seek to influence the other to change, but that goal is secondary to the goal of mutual understanding. If I love you and seek what is best for you, I am compelled to share with you what I have found to be most valuable in my life. But my effort to influence you in this way must always treat you as an authentic person, a unique individual. I must never cross the line and treat you as an object to be manipulated.[8]

Authentic dialogue is person-risking. When you really open up and share yourself with another person, that experience changes you. It may be that you come away from a dialogue thinking, "I really am glad that I do not see the world the way that person does!" But even that is change. Something about human nature makes us fear change. Instead of engaging in authentic dialogue, we usually engage in what Eric Berne called "small talk," "pastimes," "rituals" and "games."[9] Authentic dialogue requires a level of transparency that we may find uncomfortable. When we really open ourselves to another person, we become vulnerable. But because of the very fact that authentic dialogue is person-risking, it is also person-making. That is what real education is all about. That is how we become fully-functioning persons.

## Authentic Dialogue

Some fundamental principles must be understood for authentic dialogue to take place along with some important practices. Authentic dialogue does not happen by accident. It is something two people do on purpose. The following principles are prerequisites to authentic dialogue.

## Authentic Dialogue Principles

### 1. Authentic dialogue begins with a firm conviction that absolute truth is possible, knowable and propositional.

If there were no such thing as objective truth that can be understood and that can be expressed in the propositions of ordinary language, there would be no reason to engage in dialogue. If the only truth is my subjective truth and your subjective truth, a dialogue would not give either of us a reason to change.

If you ask postmodernists if they are really sure that no truth is absolute, knowable and propositional, they will answer, "Absolutely!" The only thing they are absolutely sure about is that there is no absolute truth. Their statement, of course, is self-contradictory. It is a statement of an absolute truth. It is stated as something that can be known. And it is stated in propositional form.

Postmodernism leaves us with no guidance we can trust. Modernism, however, went too far in the opposite direction. Modernism confidently affirmed that the scientific method would give us all the guidance we needed. Those who accepted modernism believed that information produces certainty. A more accurate view, in my opinion, is that information reduces uncertainty.

Study what the Bible says about things we can know:

- John 8:32: "[Y]ou will know the truth, and the truth will set you free."
- Ephesians 3:4: "When you read this, you can perceive my insight into the mystery of Christ."
- Ephesians 5:17: "[D]o not be foolish, but understand what the will of the Lord is."
- 1 John 2:21: "I write to you, not because you do not know the truth, but because you know it, and because no lie is of the truth."
- 1 John 5:13: "I write these things to you who believe in the name of the Son of God that you may know that you have eternal life."

Study what the Bible teaches about humility:

- Proverbs 16:18-19: "Pride goes before destruction, and a haughty spirit before a fall. It is better to be of a lowly spirit with the poor than to divide the spoil with the proud."
- Proverbs 29:23: "One's pride will bring him low, but he who is lowly in spirit will obtain honor."
- Isaiah 55:8-9: "For my thoughts are not your thoughts, neither are your ways my ways, declares the LORD. For as the heavens are higher than the earth, so are my ways higher than your ways and my thoughts than your thoughts."
- Micah 6:8: "He has told you, O man, what is good; and what does the LORD require of you but to do justice, and to love kindness, and to walk humbly with your God?"
- Matthew 5:3: "Blessed are the poor in spirit, for theirs is the kingdom of heaven."
- Matthew 23:12: "Whoever exalts himself will be humbled, and whoever humbles himself will be exalted."
- Romans 11:33-36: "Oh, the depth of the riches and wisdom and knowledge of God! How unsearchable are his judgments and how inscrutable his ways! 'For who has known the mind of the Lord, or who has been his counselor? Or who has given a gift to him that he might be repaid?' For from him and through him and to him are all things. To him be glory forever. Amen."
- Colossians 3:12: "Put on then, as God's chosen ones, holy and beloved, compassionate hearts, kindness, humility, meekness, and patience."
- James 4:6: "God opposes the proud, but gives grace to the humble."
- James 4:10: "Humble yourselves before the Lord, and he will exalt you."

Such a study as this should clearly show that we can know enough to be confident about what we must do to be saved and to have the kind of oneness that God requires. But we should also be humble enough to admit that we do not know everything. Have you ever said that every time you read through the Bible you find something new? That must mean that you did not know it all earlier.

2. Dialogue requires that those involved be humble enough to admit that they do not know everything and that they might be able to learn from what their partners in dialogue have to share with them.

When you and I differ, it is possible that I am totally right and you are totally wrong – or that you are totally right and I am totally wrong. It is also possible that we are both wrong, but we differ because we are wrong in different ways. What is not possible is that both of us are totally right. What is most likely, however, is that both of us may be partially right but differ in our understanding because we know different parts of God's absolute truth.

A good illustration of this is the poem by John Godfrey Saxe titled "The Blind Men and the Elephant" when the six blind men of Hindustan described an elephant. One blind man fell against the side of the elephant and said that an elephant is like a wall. A second blind man felt the elephant's tusk and concluded that it was a spear. A third man examined the elephant's trunk and told the others that an elephant is like a big snake. The fourth blind man felt the elephant's knee and thought it was a tree. The fifth blind man felt its ear and thought it was a fan. The sixth blind man felt the elephant's tail and concluded that it was a rope. A Postmodernist reading this story would conclude that there is no such thing as a real elephant – just several very different perceptions. I believe that a real elephant actually exists because God sees the whole elephant and not a part.

Humility before God compels us to recognize that when we read the Bible we have our perceptions of God's absolute truth but not absolute truth itself. Remember, I believe that absolute truth is possible, knowable and propositional. What I do not believe is that I have absolutely perfect understanding of God's absolute truth. There is always a potential difference between God's absolute truth and my perception of that truth. Therefore, I must always be open to correction and to additional learning that brings me closer to God's absolute truth.

Once at a seminar where I was discussing these things, a brother insisted that "We do not interpret Scripture; we just read it and obey." To prove his point, he read 2 Peter 1:20 in the King James Version, "[N]o prophecy of the Scripture is of any private interpretation." But even in the King James Version, verse 21 makes it clear that the subject here is the origin of prophecy and not what is involved when we read it or hear it. Interpretation is essential. Without interpretation there is no understanding at all.

Another brother thought he could trap me on the two horns of a dilemma. He asked, "Was God: (a) unable or (b) unwilling to communicate with us in such a way that we could understand perfectly?" I told him that "the correct answer was (c) neither of the above." The problem is not with the ability or the willingness of God. The problem is with the limitations of our human nature. I cannot be perfect in my understanding because I am not God. One other brother then said, "If I am wrong on any subject, you show me where!" I replied, "How about humility?"

### 3. Authentic dialogue requires that each accept the other without judging.

Non-judgmental acceptance does not mean approval. Sharing the experience of such a dialogue is a kind of fellowship, but it does not mean approval. The New Testament Greek word for "fellowship" is translated as "sharing," "having in common," "communication," "partnership," and "communion," but it is never translated as "approval." Fellowship in an activity would seem to imply approval of the activity, but it does not imply approval of the people who share that activity with you. I may judge some doctrine that you hold to be wrong without passing judgment on your eternal destiny. Our dialogue can go on while we leave it up to God to pronounce the final judgment. In my classes at Harding University when I tried to teach my students about this, I asked them to get a sheet of paper and draw a line down the middle. Then I asked them to list on one side of that line all of the positive references to judging that they can find in the Scriptures. I told them to omit positive references of God's judging. We already know that it is acceptable for God to judge. They are just supposed to list positive references to a kind of judging that people do. On the other side of that line, I ask them to list all of the negative references to judging that they can find in the Bible. To simplify the assignment, I ask them to limit their search to New Testament passages.

Here are some of the positive references to judging:

- Luke 12:57: "And why do you not judge for yourselves what is right?"

- John 7:24: "Do not judge by appearances, but judge with right judgment."
- 1 Corinthians 5:3: "For though absent in body, I am present in spirit; and as if present, I have already pronounced judgment on the one who did such a thing."
- 1 Corinthians 5:12: "Is it not those inside the church whom you are to judge?"
- 1 Corinthians 6:1-6 (where the reference is to a kind of judging involved in settling a dispute between brethren): "Is it so, that there is not a wise man among you, not even one, who will be able to judge between his brethren? But brother goes to law against brother, and that before unbelievers!" (vv. 5-6 NKJV).
- 1 Corinthians 10:15: "[J]udge for yourselves what I say."
- 1 Corinthians 11:13: "Judge for yourselves … "

Here are some of the negative references to judging:

- Matthew 7:1-5: (The context here shows that the reference is to fault-finding.) "Judge not, that you be not judged" (v. 1).
- Luke 6:37: "Judge not, and you will not be judged; condemn not, and you will not be condemned."John 5:22: "The Father judges no one, but has given all judgment to the Son."
- John 7:24: "Do not judge by appearances, but judge with right judgment."
- 1 Corinthians 10:29: "For why should my liberty be determined by someone else's conscience?"
- Colossians 2:16-18: "Therefore let no one pass judgment on you … Let no one disqualify you."
- James 4:11-12: "But who are you to judge your neighbor?" (v. 12).
- Romans 14-15: The brother who eats meat with a clear conscience must not look down on the brother whose conscience will not permit him to eat meat. But the brother who does not eat meat must not judge the brother who does. This discussion ends with this admonition, "Therefore welcome one another as Christ has welcomed you, for the glory of God" (15:7). Christ did not accept you or me on the basis of our perfect understanding or our perfect obedience. He accepted us on the basis of our trust in him.

The conclusion based on these positive and negative references to judging seems obvious to me. Christians should judge to distinguish between truth and error, right and wrong, or good and evil. It is acceptable for Christians to judge to settle disputes between or among brethren. Christians must judge the conduct of other Christians who sin and refuse to repent in spite of repeated admonitions. Christians must judge doctrines and practices. But we are not supposed to judge the heart, the motives or the eternal destiny of another person. We must leave it to God to pronounce the final judgment.

Some of my brethren who share my interest in promoting more evangelism are afraid that Christians will not be evangelistic unless they first make a judgment about which of their relatives and friends are already saved and which ones are still lost in sin and headed for eternal damnation. They are concerned about Christians who "cannot tell who is saved and who is lost." I understand their concern, and I recognize that we cannot avoid reaching some tentative conclusions about who is saved and who is lost. We could say to another person, "If my understanding of the Bible is correct, there may be some question about your spiritual condition." We can invite such people to study the Bible with us. We can let the Bible be the teacher and both of us be the students. We can share with each other our faith, our insights and our understanding of the Scriptures. That kind of authentic non-manipulative dialogue can help us both come closer to a mature understanding of God's absolute truth. We enter such a dialogue with the hope that the other person will learn from what we have to share with him or her, but we open ourselves to the possibility that we may learn from what he or she has to share with us.

Is it possible that God's grace may cover intellectual errors? I believe that it is. If it were not, there would be no hope for any of us. Is it possible for erring brethren to be saved? I hope so. Erring brethren are the only kind of brethren we have. That is the human condition. Salvation is not based on getting a grade of 100 percent on the doctrine exam. That does not mean that doctrine is unimportant. Doctrine is just what the Word of God teaches. Grace must never be used as an excuse for failing to correct known errors in our lives or in our understanding of God's will.

So begin with the confidence that truth can be known. Begin with the humility to admit that you do not know it all. You just might be able to learn from what another person has to share with you. Accept your partner in dialogue without judging. Judge doctrines and practices, but leave it up to God to pronounce the final judgment regarding our eternal destiny.

## Authentic Dialogue Practices

It is much easier to list the practices involved in an authentic dialogue than it is to actually do these things. I have often discussed these practices while engaged with couples in marriage counseling. I have also talked about these same practices when consulting with a church regarding conflict management. When I have done either of these things, it has usually taken a long time to explain each of these points. It has taken even longer for those involved to learn how to develop these skills and put them into practice. I simply list the practices here and leave it to the reader to meditate on each of them.

1. Listen to understand others, not just to find flaws in what they say.
2. Look for similarities between another person's position and yours before you look for differences.
3. Clarify differences by stating the other person's position in a way that will be acceptable to him or her.
4. Try to fit another person's way of seeing things into your personal perspective.
5. Recognize that we do not hold all beliefs with an equal degree of certainty.
6. Instead of attacking in an effort to prove the other person to be wrong, simply offer an explanation of what you believe and why you believe it. There is no room for arguing in an authentic dialogue. There is plenty of room for argument in the logical sense of explaining why you believe what you believe. There is room for an explanation of why you cannot accept the other person's way of seeing things. But that kind of explanation is a gift rather than a personal attack.
7. Do not use a bad argument to "prove" something you believe to be true. There may be some lines of reasoning that support your position that you know are not valid. Do not use them.
8. If you know of an argument against your personal position that

your partner in dialogue does not know, share it and answer it as best you can. A one-sided argument that fails to recognize and deal with counter arguments is effective only when: (1) the people in the audience have less than high school education; (2) they are not likely to hear the counter-argument from another source; and (3) all that you are trying to achieve is temporary attitude change.

9. Do not use emotional appeal until after you have laid the proper foundation by teaching God's will so that the other person knows it and you know that he or she knows it. It is inherently manipulative to use emotional appeal before building that kind of logical foundation.
10. Avoid all strategies that get people more ego-involved with their position. Name-calling, ridicule, attacks on personal consistency, the "dangerous trend" or "slippery slope" argument, insult and abuse – all of these get people more ego-involved with their position on an issue. If that happens, they are likely to exaggerate the difference between their position and yours. They are likely to minimize the similarity between their position and yours. That makes compromise much less likely.
11. Admit ownership of your perceptions and be willing to explain why you believe what you believe. Don't be like those who drop a bombshell and walk off and leave it – those who say, "It is not an issue" and refuse to explain their views. On the other hand, don't be like those who use raw political power, intimidation or threats to get their way without ever explaining why they see things as they do.
12. When dealing with disputes between or among brethren, do not try to resolve differences by deciding who gets their way. That is the approach of competition, and what you need is collaboration. Work toward a compromise that is acceptable to all involved. That makes the compromise a "win-win" situation.
13. When dealing with disputes between or among members of the same congregation, if you cannot agree, see if there is some way to avoid intruding your disagreement into the shared experience of your congregation.
14. If you cannot in good conscience worship together in the same congregation, let your separation be based on your conscience and not on your judgment of one another.

## Conclusion

The principles and practices discussed in this chapter have application in many areas. This is the way evangelism and church leadership should be done. Many of these things are used regularly in marriage and family therapy.

If someone had communicated in this way with the people who left Churches of Christ, some of them might not have left. But the main reason that I included this discussion about authentic dialogue is that this is the spirit in which I want to respond to those open-ended essays in the "Why I Left Churches of Christ" survey. Those essays and my responses will be the focus of the rest of this book.

As you read the following chapters, you will find that my personal reflections are much longer than the quoted material from the essay responses. It may seem that I have used material from those essays as an excuse for discussing some things that I believed needed to be discussed. I admit that such a perception may be accurate. My main concern, however, is that some readers may think that these 325 who left Churches of Christ are representative of all who have left Churches of Christ. My personal opinion is that some of the things in these essay responses may reflect some of the concerns of some others who have left Churches of Christ. That is all that I can claim. So please just read these personal reflections for whatever they may or may not be worth to you. My hope and prayer is that you will find something of value in this material.

Chapter 4

# Doctrinal Differences and Misunderstandings

Some of the people who responded to the "Why I Left Churches of Christ" survey had real doctrinal differences. Others either misunderstood the doctrines taught by Churches of Christ or the congregations they attended were not at all typical of Churches of Christ throughout the United States. This chapter will begin with some things that were said about Churches of Christ that are not accurate perceptions of what most of us really believe.

It is important to remember that Churches of Christ exist and function as an informal fellowship of independent congregations with no formal written creed and no central denominational headquarters with the power to impose conformity. Given this structure – or lack of structure – the amazing thing is that 76 percent of the congregations with 87 percent of the members are similar enough to one another that no significant barriers to fellowship exist among them. Even in the larger fellowship of "mainstream" congregations there are individual differences. It may be that what these former members said about Churches of Christ were accurate perceptions of what they observed in one congregation. But they are not accurate descriptions of what most Churches of Christ teach and practice.

In the following material the former members do not always tell in their own words the stories of what they experienced although that will be the usual practice throughout this book. In the first part of this chapter, some of the section headings summarize what many of them said about why they left the Churches of Christ.

## "Churches of Christ Believe They Are the Only Ones Going to Heaven"

A few of the people who responded to this survey mentioned the false perception that members of the Churches of Christ believe we are the only ones going to heaven. Although that is one of the most common things one hears about Churches of Christ, I have not personally known of any congregation where that was taught. I have known of only a few individual members who had that belief. In one place where I preached, one of the older members said, "I know that we are not supposed to say that we are the only people going to heaven, but that's really is true, isn't it?" I tried to correct this brother.

One of the characteristics of sects is that they judge all other believers to be lost. What they claim, in effect, is, "Unless you agree with me on all issues that I define as essential, you cannot be saved." That kind of judging is wrong. But an opposite extreme is characteristic of most denominations today. They judge other believers to be saved in spite of what they see as serious errors in what others teach and practice. A middle ground between the sectarian and denominational extremes teaches what we understand the Bible to teach and leaves the judging to God.

Every time I have read through the Bible I have discovered something I had never noticed before. That must mean I did not yet understand everything perfectly. I certainly do not want to be like the man who said, "There is only one person in all the world who is right on all doctrinal issues, and I didn't get that way until the last time I changed my mind." Every time I find an answer to one question, I discover two or three new questions. The real mark of educated people is not how much they know but rather how aware they are of how much they do not know.

Will God's grace cover intellectual errors? It must or no one would be saved. That being the case, my personal belief is that when we get to heaven we may be surprised to see others we did not really expect to see in heaven – and they may be even more surprised to see us.

## "Churches of Christ Do Not Believe in Salvation by Grace Through Faith"

Here is what one former member wrote:

> I left Churches of Christ because I got tired of the "Yes but" approach to the doctrine of salvation by grace. When preachers or Bible class teachers mentioned grace they always said "Of course we all know that we are saved by grace – but we are not saved wholly by grace. Works are also essential." In the Church of Christ that I attended the doctrine was that grace is needed to forgive the sins we committed before we were baptized, but after that it is our obedience that keeps us in a saved condition. And when the preacher or Bible class teacher mentioned the doctrine of salvation by faith, they always had to add that we are not saved by faith alone. In fact, James 2:24 is the only place where the Bible used the expression "faith alone" and it plainly says that we are not justified by faith alone.

There may be a few Churches of Christ where that position is what one hears, but that is not what most of us believe. I have heard a few preachers complain about congregations where a preacher who mentioned grace two Sundays in a row would be branded as a liberal. A friend of mine first heard about "the Grace Issue" when he enrolled in a very conservative school preparing for ministry as a preacher. He heard other students talking about someone who was "wrong on the grace issue," but he did not know what that issue was. Because he did not want to display his ignorance, he kept his mouth shut and listened. Eventually he learned. If you believe in grace, that is the issue.

My personal understanding is that from God's standpoint salvation is wholly by grace. We do not earn any part of it. Our response to God's grace is essential to receive the free gift of salvation, but that response involves works of obedience and not works of merit. That, I believe, is what most Churches of Christ teach.

Titus 3:5 plainly says that we are not saved by works of righteousness we have done: "[H]e saved us, not because of works done by us in righteousness, but according to his own mercy, by the washing of regeneration and renewal of the Holy Spirit." This "washing" obviously refers to baptism. The note on this verse in the NIV Study Bible reflects the typical view of evangelical denominations that "It cannot mean that baptism is necessary for regeneration, since the New Testament plainly teaches that the new birth is an act of God's Spirit (see John 3:5) and is not effected or achieved by ceremony." But what this note ignores is that they have just said that the "washing of rebirth and renewal by the Holy Spirit" refers to baptism and the earlier part of this verse plainly shows that baptism is not a work of merit but is only a work of obedience. Most Churches of Christ I know teach that baptism is not why we are saved. Grace is why we are saved. Baptism is not how we are saved. It is only our faith that God counts for righteousness. But baptism is when we are saved (Galatians 3:26-27; Romans 6:3-6).

## "Churches of Christ Teach That We Cannot Know That We Are Saved"

Churches of Christ reject Calvin's doctrine of "Once saved always saved." Our salvation is based on our union with Christ, and that union can be severed (Galatians 5:4). But a doctrine of "If saved, barely saved" is just as wrong. We are saved by the perpetual cleansing power of the blood of Christ. His blood paid the ransom price that forgave all our sins – past, present and future. As long as our union with Christ remains, we are saved in spite of our imperfection. It is only if and when we turn away from Christ that we fall from grace. Christians, therefore, can know that we are saved. If any Churches of Christ teach otherwise, they are wrong. If we had to be perfect in our obedience to remain in a saved condition, there would be no hope for any of us. We are not saved by being "good enough." God does not weigh our sins on one side of the scales and our good deeds on the other side – as many people assume. We are saved by grace through faith (Ephesians 2:8-9). That is what the Bible teaches and what most Churches of Christ believe.

## "Churches of Christ Do Not Believe in the Indwelling of the Holy Spirit"

Some of the responses to this survey came from people who thought that Churches of Christ do not believe in the indwelling of the Holy Spirit. In a large majority of Churches of Christ, it is not the indwelling of the Holy Spirit that is rejected. What is rejected is Calvin's doctrine that people are saved by a direct operation of the Holy Spirit totally separate and apart from the influence of God's Word.

Calvinism starts with a doctrine of original sin (hereditary total depravity). According to Calvin, humans are born with a totally corrupt nature. We could not believe even if we wanted to, and we cannot want to. Before people can believe, God must work a miracle changing their hearts. That miraculous experience of grace is irresistible. Christ's atonement is limited to those individuals who are predestined to receive this miraculous conversion. And once people have been saved by the miraculous operation of the Holy Spirit, they could never fall from grace. Denominations classified as "evangelical" accept all or at least significant parts of Calvin's doctrines. Churches of Christ and the other heirs of the Stone-Campbell Restoration Movement reject all of these doctrines.

Churches of Christ do not believe that people are born good. We have to learn to be good. But we are born with the power of free will. When we mature, we are capable of understanding and obeying the message of the gospel. Faith comes from hearing the word (Romans 10:17), not from a miraculous operation of the Holy Spirit apart from the Word.

Most Churches of Christ believe that when we are baptized we receive the forgiveness of our sins and the gift of the Holy Spirit's indwelling. Some claim that in Acts 2:38 the Holy Spirit is the giver and forgiveness of our sins is the gift. But it is clear that God is the giver, and the Holy Spirit is the gift (5:32). It is important to note that every blessing the Bible attributes to the indwelling of the Holy Spirit the Bible also attributes to the influence of the inspired Word as recorded in the Scriptures.

This indwelling is not totally separate from the Word, but it is more than a matter of memorizing Bible verses. Just before baptism, people do not yet have the indwelling of the Holy Spirit. Just after baptism they do. But they did not memorize any Bible verses while they were under the water. What happens at baptism is that the Word which had been a part of what we knew was put into action by our obedience. What changes at the point of baptism is how God sees us. The change is not in the physical part of us but in the spiritual part. The Holy Spirit starts the life-long process of transforming our lives so that day by day we became more and more like Christ. Churches of Christ believe that the indwelling Holy Spirit empowers us and guides us but never in a way contrary to the written Word. Divine providence opens and closes doors of opportunity. God gives different gifts to us. In all these and many other ways, the Holy Spirit directs us in ways we do not always understand. But members of the Churches of Christ tend to be very skeptical of claims concerning any new revelation from God or people today having supernatural powers or miraculous guidance. I have heard preachers say, "The Lord laid this burden on my heart," or "God told me to give this message to you," when I would not have blamed God for the sermon that followed. Personally, I tend to be somewhat skeptical when someone says, "The Holy Spirit called me to go do mission work in such-and-such a place" – especially if they expect me to pay their way and give a salary to support them in the effort. I can look back throughout my life and see ways in which I am now confident that God was leading me. But instead of placing all the responsibility on God for the decision, I prefer to use the kind of language that Luke used in Acts 16:9-10: "And a vision appeared to Paul in the night: a man of Macedonia was standing there, urging him and saying, 'Come over to Macedonia and help us.' And when Paul had seen the vision, immediately we sought to go on into Macedonia, concluding that God had called us to preach the gospel to them." We should pray as though it all depends on God because it does. But we should make the most rational decision we can as though it all depends on us because it does. God guides us through our rational thought processes.

My personal understanding is that the Holy Spirit sometimes guides us by helping us to remember a relevant passage of Scripture. In the prayer just before the sermon, I have often had people pray that the Lord would give me a "ready recollection" of the things I had prepared to say.

Why is it that when we pray for God to guide us, we remember one

Bible verse and not another? I usually wake up in the morning with a song in my thoughts – some familiar hymn. But why one song and not another? I believe that the Holy Spirit can guide us through things like that. But we have to use our rational thought processes to decide whether this was God's guidance or something random with no meaning at all. Recently, I woke up hearing the radio alarm playing an old song that had something to do with a witch doctor telling someone what to do. The witch doctor sang something like, "Ooo, Eee, Ooo, Ahh, Ahh, Ting Tang Walla Walla Bing Bang." I did not take that to be divine guidance. Or if I woke up with four Bible verses going through my consciousness: "[Judas] went and hanged himself"; "You go, and do likewise"; "What you are going to do, do quickly"; and "I tell you, there will be more joy in heaven" (Matthew 27:5; Luke 10:37; John 13:27; Luke 15:7) – I would not call that a message from the Holy Spirit. The Lord can guide us through the things that come into our conscious awareness at different times, but we must decide what meaning, if any, to attribute to those memories.

Perhaps that is what J.B.F. Wright had in mind when he wrote the words and the music to the old hymn "Precious Memories." He seemed to think that memories that come to our conscious awareness can be, as he wrote, "Sent from somewhere to my soul."

That may also have been what Septimus Winner (who usually published his songs under the name Alice Hawthorne) was thinking about when he wrote the words to the old hymn "Whispering Hope." In this song, hope is represented as a divine message that sustains us in times of trial.

**Whispering Hope (1868)**

Soft as the voice of an angel, Breathing a lesson unheard,
Hope with a gentle persuasion, Whispers her comforting word;
Wait till the darkness is over, Wait till the tempest is done,
Hope for the sunshine tomorrow, After the shower is gone.

If, in the dusk of the twilight, Dim be the region afar,
Will not the deepening darkness, Brighten the glimmering star?
Then when the night is upon us, Why should the heart sink away?
When the dark midnight is over, Watch for the breaking of day.

Hope, as an anchor so steadfast, Rends the dark veil for the soul,
Whither the Master has entered, Robbing the grave of its goal.
Come, then O come, glad fruition, Come to my sad weary heart.
Come, O Thou blest hope of glory, Never, O never depart.

Whispering hope, Oh how welcome thy voice,
Making my heart in its sorrow rejoice.

These speculations of mine about how the Holy Spirit indwells and guides us are not shared by all members of the Churches of Christ. But we are united in the belief that the Holy Spirit really does dwell within us and guide us. And we do not have to understand the manner to accept the fact of the Holy Spirit's indwelling and guidance.

This approach is far too rational for those who say, "I would not trade a whole stack of Bibles for the feeling deep down in my heart." My question for those who interpret their feelings to be messages from God is this: How do you know that the feeling came from the Holy Spirit and not from Satan?

The fact that this approach seems to be "too rational" may be why some people think that members of the Churches of Christ do not believe in the indwelling of the Holy Spirit. Some went so far away from Calvinism and Pentecostalism that they adopted a "Word Only" doctrine that limited the Holy Spirit's indwelling to nothing more than the influence of the Bible in our lives.

## An Issue Concerning Bible Versions

One of the youth ministers who left Churches of Christ mentioned an issue concerning Bible versions. Here is a part of what he wrote:

> In the congregation where I served as a youth minister, the elders made a rule against using any translation of the Bible other than the King James Version in Bible classes, preaching or public Scripture reading. A church consultant conducted an anonymous survey of our congregation. That survey had more than 100 items. One asked for levels of agreement or disagreement with the statement: "The King James Version of the Bible is the only version that should be

> used in Bible classes, preaching or public Scripture reading." Only 5 percent of the members said "Agree" or "Strongly Agree" with that statement. But some of that small minority were very vocal, and it included some big contributors. That restriction made it very difficult for me to work with young people. The King James Version has a 12th grade reading level, and most college students do not read at that level.

The "King James Only" position is not at all typical in Churches of Christ. Most members of the Churches of Christ understand that no translation is perfect. Translations are not inspired and do not claim to be. The King James Version has errors. Serious students of the Bible study several different translations.

## Examples of Real Doctrinal Differences

Eight of the 325 who responded to the "Why I Left Churches of Christ" survey converted to non-Christian religions: two to Judaism, two to Buddhism, one joined Wicca and another described himself as a pagan. Those who have accepted these other belief systems would not likely return to Churches of Christ even in a congregation that became so politically correct, open-minded and tolerant it would welcome people who no longer believe in Christ. Such a church, of course, would have no valid reason to exist.

Among those who responded to this survey, 127 said they had no religious affiliation. Twenty-four of these included the information that they no longer believe in God or at least that they no longer believe in the deity of Jesus. In an effort to win back these unbelievers, Churches of Christ could become the social equivalent of a church for the unbelievers. But most unbelievers feel no need for such a fellowship. If Churches of Christ changed in that way, why would they even want to exist?

The doctrinal differences mentioned most often in this survey involved something that is not as central in our belief system as things like the existence of God and the deity of Jesus Christ. But the difference about one issue is real. That issue involves the use of instrumental music in the worship assemblies of the church. Fifty-three of those who left joined Christian Churches. The most obvious difference is that the Christian

Churches use instrumental music, and most Churches of Christ do not. Fifty-three others who left Churches of Christ joined independent community-type churches. There is such diversity among independent community-type churches that I cannot be sure about all of them. But all of those I know about use instrumental music, although they differ from Churches of Christ in a good many other ways. The 84 others went to 23 different religious groups.[1] I have devoted one entire chapter in this book, Chapter 10, to the instrumental music issue. But that was not because of the inherent importance of the issue. Instead, it was because of how frequently that issue was mentioned in the survey results.

A doctrinal difference that was mentioned by just a few who responded to this study provides a good example of how compromise on one issue could have profound implications. That issue is in regard to what Churches of Christ teach about homosexual behavior. The rest of this chapter is devoted to a study of that issue.

## What Churches of Christ Teach About Homosexual Behavior

One former member wrote: "I was born gay and finally realized it when I was 18 years old. The Church of Christ would not accept my lifestyle, so I left."

Only six of the 325 responses to this survey reflected the homosexual agenda. Four of these came from former members who said that although they do not have a homosexual orientation, they strongly object to the doctrine of Churches of Christ teaching that homosexual behavior is contrary to the will of God. In some of the more "progressive" Churches of Christ where I have helped to interpret survey results, a small but vocal minority has expressed views that reflect the so-called "gay rights" agenda. They want Churches of Christ to be more politically correct. They urge their local congregation to adopt a more tolerant and inclusive posture by welcoming practicing homosexuals into full fellowship.

The young man quoted earlier admitted engaging in homosexual activity with multiple partners. That is what he called his "lifestyle." It was an ongoing pattern of behavior. He claimed that he was born with this homosexual orientation. He wrote, "Because God made me this way, it must be acceptable to God for me to express my sexuality in this way." A similar response came from a woman who said that she was in "a long-term, committed lesbian relationship." She said that she has always been a lesbian; she was born that way. She also said that she left because Churches of Christ did not approve of her relationship. She wanted Churches of Christ to stop condemning homosexual behavior. But changing that doctrine would require rejecting a more fundamental doctrine regarding the full inspiration and final authority of the Bible.

## The Biblical Background of the Term "Sodomy"

The term "sodomy" is used in several ways. It is primarily applied to men having sexual intercourse with other men. Occasionally it is defined more broadly to include lesbianism – women having sexual intercourse with other women. In the laws of some states, "sodomy" is defined in a narrower way and is limited to oral sex, whether in a heterosexual or homosexual relationship. Actually the term comes from a biblical reference.

In the ancient city of Sodom, two angels came in the form of men to warn Lot and his family to flee before God destroyed the city. "[T]he men of the city, the men of Sodom, both young and old, all the people to the last man, surrounded the house. And they called to Lot, 'Where are the men who came to you tonight? Bring them out to us, that we may know them' " (Genesis 19:4-5). The word "know" is used here in the same way as the word "knew" in Genesis 4:1: "Now Adam knew Eve his wife, and she conceived and bore Cain." The sin of Sodom was not a lack of hospitality toward strangers, as some have suggested. The men of Sodom wanted to have sexual intercourse with these "men," not knowing that they were angels in human form. The nature of this behavior is clearly seen in Leviticus 18:22: "You shall not lie with a male as with a woman; it is an abomination." Sexual intercourse is "sodomy" when the relationship is between two men or between two women. The seriousness of this offense is seen in the previous context of verses 6-18 where various forms of incest are prohibited, verse 20 where adultery is forbidden and verse 21 in which human sacrifice of infants was forbidden. Then in the following context, verse 23 condemns bestiality: "And you shall not lie with any animal and so make yourself unclean with it, neither shall any woman give herself to an animal to lie with it: it is perversion." The rest of Leviticus 18 explains that these acts done by the people would cause God to drive them out of the land He promises to give to the people of Israel. But God said if the people of Israel engaged in the same practices, He would drive them out of that land.

The law in Leviticus 20:13 commanded: "If a man lies with a male as with a woman, both of them have committed an abomination; they shall surely be put to death; their blood is upon them." Some defenders of homosexual behavior have argued that since homosexual behavior under the new covenant would not receive a death penalty, it must now be regarded as acceptable to God. But that claim is refuted by what Paul wrote in Romans 1:24-27 concerning people who knew God but refused to glorify him as God:

> Therefore God gave them up in the lusts of their hearts to impurity, to the dishonoring of their bodies among themselves, because they exchanged the truth about God for a lie and worshiped and served the creature rather than the Creator, who is blessed forever! Amen. For this reason God gave them up to dishonorable passions. For their women exchanged natural relations for those that are contrary to nature; and the men likewise gave up natural relations with women and were consumed with passion for one another, men committing shameless acts with men and receiving in themselves the due penalty for their error.

God does not hate people who have a homosexual orientation. What he forbids is homosexual behavior. In 1 Corinthians 6:9-11, Paul wrote:

> Or do you not know that the unrighteous will not inherit the kingdom of God? Do not be deceived: neither the sexually immoral, nor idolaters, nor adulterers, nor men who practice homosexuality, nor thieves, nor the greedy, nor drunkards, nor revilers, nor swindlers will inherit the kingdom of God. And such were some of you. But you were washed, you were sanctified, you were justified in the name of the Lord Jesus Christ and by the Spirit of our God.

People who are attracted to members of the same sex can become Christians. However, they must repent and stop engaging in homosexual behavior. As far as I can tell, the jury is still out on the question of whether the right kind of therapy can change a person's sexual orientation. But it is clear that becoming a Christian can change behavior. If therapy does not change their sexual orientation, they can live celibate lives that glorify God. Paul and Barnabas lived celibate lives, and Paul saw some spiritual advantages in that kind of life (1 Corinthians 7:1-7).

## Is a Homosexual Orientation Inborn?

Before leaving this subject, I want to address briefly the claim of the young man who responded to this survey with the claim that he was born homosexual. The homosexual community has tried to find scientific evidence that homosexual orientations are inborn. If such evidence is ever found, that still would not show that God approves of homosexual behavior. It would only indicate that God has called some people to a celibate life. But I do not believe that homosexual orientation is inborn.

When I was studying for a psychology degree at the University of Houston, I had a course on "The Psychology of Human Sexuality" with Dr. James Leslie McCary, the author of a classic text that students called "More than anyone ever wanted to know or cared to ask about sex."[2] McCary, as far as I know, never claimed to be a Christian or even a believer in God. He held very liberal views on the legalization of homosexual behavior. For example he wrote, "If this behavior is not harmful to the participants, is carried out by consenting adults without any sort of coercion, and is out of sight and sound of unwilling observers, it should be considered acceptable, whether or not others would care to participate in similar acts."[3] McCary had little to say in his book regarding the origin of a homosexual orientation. But in class one day someone asked, "Do you believe that some people are born with a homosexual orientation?" His answer was, "No. People are not born homosexual or heterosexual. They are just born sexual. They are born with a capacity to respond sexually. However, sexual orientations are learned. There may be some predisposing factors, but people learn how to respond sexually."

There is, I believe, a parallel in alcoholism. There is good scientific evidence to show that some people are born with a physical predisposition to become alcoholics. Just a few drinks are enough for them to become addicted. Others come from family situations that psychologically may predispose them to alcoholism. But the reality is that alcohol is what makes alcoholics. Those who never take the first drink never become addicted to alcohol. In much the same way, some people may be predisposed to develop a homosexual orientation. Through engaging in homosexual behavior people learn that orientation. This may be what Paul was writing about in Romans 1:27: "and the men likewise gave up natural relations with women and were consumed with passion for one another, men committing shameless acts with men and receiving in themselves the due penalty for their error." If you ate enough slop with the pigs, you might develop an appetite for slop and not even want to eat good nourishing food. That could be your punishment for eating slop.

Churches of Christ could follow in the path of some liberal Protestant denominations that have ordained openly "gay" clergy – including bishops. But doing so would eventually lead to the kind of church that stands for nothing and falls for everything. Being open-minded is good, but people should not become so open-minded that their brains fall out. If the responses to the "Why I Left Churches of Christ" survey are any indication, few are leaving because of the position Churches of Christ take on homosexual behavior.

There is one more point I must make on this subject. There is no justification for persecuting people with a homosexual orientation. Churches should show more compassion for people who are troubled by gender confusion. We should be careful to avoid confusing a homosexual orientation with homosexual behavior. It is the behavior that God forbids, not the orientation.

As a citizen, I am troubled by laws making homosexual marriages legal. But as a Christian, I still know what God intended marriage to be – a committed lifetime relationship between a man and a woman. Regardless of what politicians and judges may say, as a Christian I must still teach that homosexual behavior is an abomination in the sight of God. It is sin. Those who engage in such practices must repent to be saved by the grace of God.

# Lost by Neglect

A common theme was observed in many of the responses to the "Why I Left Churches of Christ" survey. The following examples are typical. Each, of course, reflects the perceptions of just one person or one family. If we could talk to the members of these congregations, they might tell a very different story. But there is probably enough reality in these stories to make them worth considering.

## Comments by Those Who Left

"When we were members of the Church of Christ, no one seemed to care whether we attended or not. When we left, no one asked why. No one visited or called." Many of the responses that did not list this as a reason for leaving at least mentioned that when they left no one asked why and no one called or visited them.

> The first few times we visited, no one spoke to us – unless we first spoke to them. The members seemed to be very friendly with one another, but they appeared to have little interest in visitors. We placed membership anyhow, but soon learned that most of the members already had their quota of friends, and they had little interest in newcomers. We tried for three years

> to make friends in this congregation without any success. We left and went to a community church where we were quickly welcomed. We now have many friends in the church we attend.

> My father was an elder in the Church of Christ for many years. He had to resign because of his health. In the last few years of his life, my mother had to stay with him 24/7. She needed the kind of help that she and my father had given to many others throughout the years. But no one offered to help. My sister and I visited as often as we could, but we both live and work so far from Mother and Dad that we could not visit very often. When Dad died, only a handful of people from the Church of Christ came to the funeral. Soon after Dad died, Mother had to go to a nursing home. Very few of the church members visited her. When she died, only two church members came to her funeral. That neglect gave me a very bad impression of Churches of Christ. My family and I are now Baptists, and our church would never treat former leaders the way those people treated my parents.

> My husband and I used to be members of the Church of Christ. Because of various health problems, we were not able to attend church services very often. When we did, few people even spoke to us. After my husband had a stroke, he was in the hospital for more than a month. The preacher visited twice. None of the elders ever came. No other members visited. After my husband came home from the hospital, we went for more than a year without going to church. Then one day we got a letter from the church signed by the new preacher for the elders. They withdrew fellowship from us because we had "forsaken the assembly." No one asked why we were no longer going to church. They just took our names out of the membership list. So really we did not leave the Church of Christ. We were kicked out!

I could go on and on for many pages with the stories of these people. But this should be enough to give you a feeling for the kind of things many former members wrote to explain why they left Churches of Christ. Because this survey was anonymous, there was no way I could contact these people. But if I could, I would tell them that Churches of Christ are not all like that. Things like this would never happen in most of the congregations I know. I would tell them how sorry I am for the way they were neglected and mistreated. I most certainly would not try to defend this kind of behavior by church members. That, of course, is not all that I would want to say, but it is where I would begin.

I really would like to talk to the people who had the fellowship of the church withdrawn from them because of their failure to attend church services. If I could, I would explain that what happened to them does not reflect the beliefs or practices of most Churches of Christ. However, I know that such things have happened. A cousin of mine was a deacon in a congregation where the elders announced to the deacons that they had a list of 50 members who had not attended church services for the past three years. The elders said that they planned to withdraw fellowship from these people the following Sunday. My cousin asked, "How are they going to notice it?" Other deacons expressed similar concerns. The elders had a hasty huddle and announced that they were going to delay the withdrawal of fellowship. In a later meeting with the deacons, the elders announced that they were going to begin a program of intense fellowshiping of these 50 members. Elders would visit in the homes of each of these members. Elders would invite these delinquent members to visit in their homes. "Then, when we withdraw fellowship they will notice it," they said. As it turned out, however, they did not get to withdraw fellowship from any of those members. Three of them had died, four had moved away, and all of the others came back to church, confessed their sins and were restored.

That true story might be amusing if it were not so sad. In the New Testament when the fellowship of the church was withdrawn from a member, it was from someone who was still a part of that fellowship and who wanted to remain in fellowship with other Christians. Furthermore, a formal withdrawal of fellowship, as outlined in 1 Corinthians 5, was a last resort. The action was taken when it was necessary to protect the influence of the church in the community and to protect the other members from the corrupting influence of members who refused to repent of their sins – such as the incestuous relationship of the man in the Corinthian church who had taken his father's wife. A third reason for taking this extreme action was to shock the offending members into a realization of their sins in the hope of bringing them to repentance (2 Thessalonians 3:14-15). Furthermore, this action always had to follow the rule of Christ given in Matthew 18:15-17. First, go to the person in private and plead for him or her to repent. If that effort fails, go back with two or three witnesses. If the person still refuses to repent, the next step would be for the elders to go to that person in the name of the whole church and urge repentance. Only if all of that fails to persuade the person to repent would there be a formal withdrawal of fellowship. And that action would be taken by the whole church, not just by the elders. It most certainly would not be done by a letter from a preacher.

If I could speak face-to-face with others who felt so neglected and isolated, I would have to go beyond expressing my sorrow for how they were treated. I would explain that they cannot put all the blame on others. They must accept responsibility for their personal decisions and actions. Getting mad at church members and expressing that anger by leaving the Lord's church is about like getting mad at the dog and kicking the cat.

## Defensive Responses of Some Members

When I have discussed the results of this survey and talked about this kind of neglect, some church members have become defensive. Here are some of their reactions:

> I go to church to worship God, and I would keep on doing that no matter how unfriendly the church members might be. Why can't they?
>
> I have never attended a congregation where I could not easily and quickly make friends. Anyone can find plenty of friends in the church if they just try.
>
> The people who leave Churches of Christ are personally responsible for what they did. They should not blame everything on others.

> John explained why some people leave: "They went out from us, but they were not of us; for if they had been of us, they would have continued with us. But they went out, that it might become plain that they all are not of us" (1 John 2:19).

When I hear these defensive responses, I try to make it clear that people are indeed responsible for their decisions and actions. They cannot blame everything on others. It is also important to note that the church is not a social club. Christianity is not just about having friends. But on the other hand, having close personal relationships with friends and relatives who are also Christians is very important. Christianity involves two kinds of relationships. There is a vertical relationship that we have with God. There is also a horizontal relationship that we have with one another: "[H]e who does not love his brother whom he has seen cannot love God whom he has not seen" (1 John 4:20).

For almost 40 years now, I have conducted seminars on evangelism, leadership and related topics for congregations throughout the United States and Canada. In almost all of these seminars I have asked people to hold up their hands if, before they became Christians, they had close personal relationships with friends or family members who were already Christians. Usually around 90 to 95 percent of the people hold up their hands. I then ask people to hold up their bands if they became Christians without first having this kind of relationship with friends or relatives who were already Christians. Usually fewer than 5 percent of the people say that they are in this category. If that is the way it is with most of us, why should we expect it to be different with others?

Several writers in the field of evangelism have used three Greek words to explain what is involved: *kerygma*, *koinonia* and *diakonia*. The *kerygma* is the message of the gospel. But some people treat evangelism as though it involved nothing more than getting people's belief systems corrected and baptizing them. What many people ignore is that, for a large majority of Christians, the *koinonia* or fellowship was the context in which they responded to the *kerygma*. And the *diakonia* is our service to others in the name of Christ that brings them into our friendship circle where they hear and respond to the gospel message.[1] But the role of the *koinonia* is not limited to disciple-making. It is also important in disciple-building. It was the koinonia that seems to have been missing in the lives of many former members who responded to this survey.

A study that I did in the early 1970s compared a sample of 50 recent adult converts who were still active members of the Churches of Christ with 50 other recent converts who had already dropped out. The people involved in both samples were asked how many friends they had made in the congregation they attended. The two groups were matched statistically based on how long they had attended a congregation of the Churches of Christ before they were interviewed or before they stopped attending. Both groups had an equal opportunity to make friends in their congregations. All who had made fewer than three friends in the church were in the "drop-out" category. All who had made seven or more friends in the church were in the category for "still active church members." [2]

## Church at Three Levels

In Peter Wagner's first book on American church growth, he wrote that people need to experience church at three levels.[3] He called these "Celebration," "Congregation" and "Cell." The church as "celebration" is the worship assembly, and there is no real limit on how large it can be. What Wagner called the church as "congregation" is something smaller than the worship assembly. It is more the size of a typical adult Bible class in a large church. What seems to work best is to start an adult Bible class with around 30 people with a commitment that when class size approached 60, they will split the class into two classes. Most of the Sunday school growth in Southern Baptist churches has come from increasing the number of classes, not from increasing class size beyond an upper limit of 60.[4]

Some interesting secular research has been done by students of group dynamics. Sixty is about the upper limit on the number of people most of us can know on a first-name basis in any organization: school, club, company or church. Cross-denominational and cross-cultural research has confirmed this upper limit of around 60. In a church with 60 members, most know all of the others on a first-name basis. In a church with 600 or 6,000 members, most will still know only 60 on a first name basis.[5]

What Wagner called the "cell" is a group of about 10 or 12 people who meet together regularly to help one another grow spiritually. Until recently, most Churches of Christ in the United States have not done anything to organize or encourage the formation of such groups. Some church leaders have even opposed the formation of such disciple-building groups. In their judgment, such groups are too much like the "prayer partner" relationships in the Crossroads/Boston Discipling Movement (since 1994 identified as the "International Churches of Christ").[6] But in groups of this size, disciple-building relationships seem to be most effective.

An organized small group ministry is relatively new, but the function is not new. When I was growing up, Christians seldom went home from Sunday morning worship services alone. We either invited others to come to our house for Sunday dinner or another family invited us to go to their home and eat. By modern standards we were poor back then; but we did not know it. We shared what we had. When others came over and ate our chickens one Sunday, we went to their house and ate their chickens the following Sunday. It all balanced out. And it was not just Sunday dinner. Our social life throughout the week was centered on getting together with other Christians. Part of the time was just used for fun and games. But we almost always sang together. I do not remember any formal organized Bible lessons in these situations, but the conversation repeatedly kept coming back to religious topics. Sometimes we argued about points of doctrine, but at least that got us into Bible study. We spent much time praying together. We were into one another's lives. When a brother or sister needed correcting, we confronted him or her and urged repentance. We held one another accountable. When others needed encouragement, we provided it. In some ways life was simpler back then, less hectic. We took time to be friends.

The comments by some who left Churches of Christ would indicate that the church has not been like that for them. That is why many Churches of Christ now have an organized small-group ministry. The need for such ministries is indicated by the results of a questionnaire study that I have done in many more than 100 congregations throughout the nation. Several related questions are listed below with the results.

1. How many close personal friends do you have in this congregation? In the average congregation, 10 percent say that they do not have any close personal friends in their congregation. Another 5 to 10 percent say that they have just one or two.
2. How many of these close personal friends did you visit in the past 12 months? For purposes of this questionnaire, "visiting" is defined as: (a) going into their home; (b) having them into your home; (c) going out and doing something together; or (d) just talking to each other regularly by telephone, e-mail, Facebook, Twitter, etc. In the average congregation, 30 percent of the members say that they have close personal friends in the church but that they have not actually visited any of them in the previous 12 months.
3. When you visit with your close personal friends in the congregation, how often do you pray together, study the Bible together, have conversations about spiritual things or do other things to help build each other up spiritually? In the average congregation, half of the members say that they have close personal friends in the church and that they have visited them in the previous 12 months – but their visiting time has been spent talking about secular things. They have not engaged in any of these disciple-building activities.
4. That leaves only 10 percent of the members who say that they have close personal friends in the congregation, that they have visited them in the previous 12 months, and that they have used part of the visiting time for disciple-building activities. The question for them is, "How often have you done this in the past 12 months?" The average response is "Less than once a month."

In reply to those who say that anyone who really wants to can make friends easily in their congregation – just as they did – I would ask them to look at their congregation through the eyes of some members who have not been assimilated. I would ask especially that they try to understand the perspective of those who have left.

Thirty years ago I conducted a church-growth seminar for a congregation that shall remain nameless to protect the guilty. I was talking about the need for a small group approach to disciple-making and disciple-building. One of the elders interrupted my lecture with this question, "If we allow the members to study their Bibles in small groups that meet in homes, how are we going to control it?" I ignored what that question implied about an authoritarian approach to church leadership. In reply, I simply said, "Do the same thing you already do with your Sunday morning Bible classes. Select good teachers. Provide good training for teachers. Provide good teaching material. And supervise the classes." Later another elder said, "I have never needed a small group to help me grow spiritually, so why should anyone else?" I reminded him that he belonged to a small group that served this function. It was called "the eldership."

## The Value of Exit Interviews

As I studied the 325 essay responses to the survey of people who have left Churches of Christ, repeatedly I read something like the comment included at the beginning of this chapter: "When we left, no one asked why. No one visited. No one called." I believe that church leaders need to have exit interviews with most members who leave. If they move away, the reason for their leaving is obvious. But do not just drop them from your membership list. Put their names in a separate file and try to keep in touch with them – at least until they have placed membership with another congregation. Send them information on congregations in the area where they have moved. Contact leaders of these congregations and tell them about church members who have moved into their area.

If they transferred membership from your congregation to another Church of Christ in the area, visit with them to ask why they left. If they joined some other religious group, ask why they left Churches of Christ. I know that such visits may be rather awkward, but you can tell them that you just want to know why they left so that you might learn now to minister better to those who have not left. Then really listen to what they say.

## "One Another" Passages

One useful kind of Bible study helps church members see the need for better relationships with other Christians. Go through the New Testament and notice all of the "one another" passages. Take a Bible that you do not mind marking with underlines or highlights or just make notes on where you find passages that use the words "one another." Notice, however, that some versions of the New Testament have "one another" language that another version does not use. But both translations indicate the importance of the relationships that Christians have with other Christians. For example, the King James Version of Romans 12:5 has "So we, being many, are one body in Christ, and every one members one of another." The language in the New International Version, 1984 is slightly different. "[S]o in Christ we who are many form one body, and each member belongs to all the others." But both translations show the importance of the connection that Christians have with other Christians.

John 13:34-35 is perhaps the most important of the "one another" passages. On the night before Jesus was crucified, he gave this command to his disciples: "A new commandment I give to you, that you love one another: just as I have loved you, you also are to love one another. By this all people will know that you are my disciples, if you have love for one another." However, most of the "one another" passages are found in Paul's letters. The following are not all of the "one another" passages in the New Testament, but they at least indicate the kinds of things Christians are told to do in their relationships with other Christians.

- "Love one another with brotherly affection. Outdo one another in showing honor" (Romans 12:10).
- "Live in harmony with one another" (Romans 12:16).
- "[W]elcome one another as Christ has welcomed you" (Romans 15:7).
- " ... instruct one another" (Romans 15:14).
- " ... through love serve one another" (Galatians 5:13).
- "Brothers, if anyone is caught in any transgression, you who are spiritual should restore him in a spirit of gentleness. Keep watch on yourself, lest you too be tempted. Bear one another's burdens, and so fulfill the law of Christ" (Galatians 6:1-2).
- " ... for we are members one of another" (Ephesians 4:25).
- "Be kind to one another, tenderhearted, forgiving one another, as God in Christ forgave you" (Ephesians 4:32).
- "submitting to one another out of reverence for Christ" (Ephesians 5:21).
- " ... as God's chosen ones, holy and beloved, compassionate

hearts, kindness, humility, meekness, and patience, bearing with one another and, if one has a complaint against another, forgiving each other; as the Lord has forgiven you, so you also must forgive. And above all these put on love, which binds everything together in perfect harmony" (Colossians 3:12-14).

- "[M]ay the Lord make you increase and abound in love for one another and for all, as we do for you" (1 Thessalonians 3:12).
- "Therefore encourage one another and build one another up" (1 Thessalonians 5:11).
- "And let us consider how to stir up one another to love and good works" (Hebrews 10:24).
- "Therefore, confess your sins to one another and pray for one another, that you may be healed" (James 5:16).
- "Finally, all of you, live in harmony with one another; be sympathetic, love as brothers, be compassionate and humble" (1 Peter 3:8 NIV1984).
- "But if we walk in the light, as he is in the light, we have fellowship with one another, and the blood of Jesus his Son cleanses us from all sin" (1 John 1:7).
- "For this is the message that you have heard from the beginning, that we should love one another" (1 John 3:11).
- "Beloved, let us love one another, for love is from God" (1 John 4:7).

In addition to these positive instructions, there are also many "one another" passages that teach what we must not do in our relationships with others. At a minimum, all of these at least imply the existence of interpersonal relationships in the lives of Christians. The following are just a few of the negative "one another" passages:

- "[L]et us not pass judgment on one another" (Romans 14:13).
- "But if you bite and devour one another, watch out that you are not consumed by one another" (Galatians 5:15).
- "Let us not become conceited, provoking one another, envying one another" (Galatians 5:26).
- "Do not lie to one another" (Colossians 3:9).
- "Do not speak evil against one another … But who are you to judge your neighbor?" (James 4:11-12).

- "Do not grumble against one another, brothers, so that you may not be judged" (James 5:9).

The bottom line of this "one another" exercise is that Christianity was not intended to be lived out in lonely isolation. The relationship that we have with other Christians is an essential part of our relationship with God.

## Where Were the Shepherds?

As I read the comment, "When I left, no one called. No one visited. No one asked why I left," it reminded me of the words of a gospel song titled "Don't Scatter the Sheep." It also reminded me of Ezekiel 34 where God condemned the unfaithful shepherds of Israel because they did not seek for the lost sheep and bring them back to the flock. They did not heal the sick ones or bind up the broken. They fed their own families but did not feed the sheep.

Here, as elsewhere throughout the Old Testament, the spiritual leaders were called "shepherds." In the New Testament, the elders of the church are also called "shepherds." It would not be appropriate to take the words of Ezekiel 34 out of context and apply them totally to elders in the church today. There are, however, some remarkable similarities and some very important lessons to learn.

Three terms were applied to the same leadership role in the New Testament. In the original Greek text, these words were *presbuteros*, *episkopos* and *poimen*. These words were translated in the Latin Vulgate, which for many centuries was the only Bible of Christendom in the West. Those Latin words eventually were translated or transliterated into English: presbyter, bishop and pastor. Modern translations generally use more common English words of Anglo-Saxon origin: elder, overseer and shepherd.

In Acts 20:17, Paul called for the elders of the church in Ephesus to meet him at the port of Miletus. In verse 28, Paul told those elders, "Pay careful attention to yourselves and to all the flock, in which the Holy Spirit has made you overseers." The overseer of a flock is a shepherd. And in the rest of verse 28, Paul used the verb form of the word for "shepherd" (*poimeno*). He told them to "care for the church of God, which he obtained with his own blood."

First Peter 5:1-3 is another place where these three terms are applied to the same leaders. Peter addressed the "elders." He told them to "shepherd the flock of God that is among you, exercising oversight."

In my book *Church Leadership and Organization,*[7] I explain how these three terms suggest three leadership functions that must be performed in any congregation:

> Elder: decision-making, policy-making, executive-type leadership focusing on strategic planning rather than day-to-day operational management;
>
> Overseer: administrative leadership supervising the work of those to whom some authority has been delegated for the day-to-day management of the church;
>
> Shepherd: spiritual counseling and teaching of the whole church and especially of individual members and their families.

Ephesians 4:11-16 explains something about how leaders produce church growth. It is not by their personal efforts. Instead, they lead by functioning in the equipping ministry. Verse 11 mentions the leaders God provided for the church: first, the apostles and prophets who gave us the written Word and spread the church throughout the world; then in local congregations, the evangelists with the "shepherds and teachers" (ESV); "pastor and teachers" (NKJV, NASB, NIV1984, ASV). Some Greek scholars claim that this can be translated "teaching shepherds" and not as two separate categories.

The role of the leaders, according to Ephesians 4:12, was "to equip the saints for the work of ministry, for building up the body of Christ." The evangelists and the teaching shepherds (or shepherds and teachers) in local congregations were supposed to help the members discover their gifts and find their ministries in the priesthood of the believers.

The result is expressed in Ephesians 4:16 (NIV1984): "From him [Christ] the whole body, joined and held together by every supporting ligament, grows and builds itself up in love, as each part does its work

The most important differences between new members who are assimilated into the congregation and those who drop out of the church are how many close personal friendships they form in the congregation, how many specific church work assignments they are given and how quickly they are involved in some area of ministry. That requires spiritual counseling and teaching of the members, one person or one family at a time.

If I were to conduct a nationwide survey among members of the Churches of Christ, I think that I would find that most church members have learned not to call their preacher the "pastor." Most, however, would not know why because they expect the preacher and any other full-time church-supported ministers on the staff to function exactly the way pastors function in the various denominations throughout the country.

Some church members have learned that in the New Testament the term "pastor" is used in reference to the elders. But in many congregations, the elders are not expected to be "teaching-shepherds." Some congregations have elders who have never even taught a Bible class. The social contract between congregations and elders simply asks these men to attend a few meetings in which they function as a decision-making body for the congregation. They especially make decisions about how to spend the money and what can or cannot be done in the church building. These elders are the ones who hire or fire the full-time church-supported ministers. But those ministers are expected to do most of the pastoral work of spiritual counseling and teaching. And often these ministers are so burdened with managing various programs they have little time for a pastoral ministry.

With these things in mind, I would encourage you to make a careful study of Ezekiel 34 and notice especially verses 2-6:

> Thus says the Lord GOD: Ah, shepherds of Israel who have been feeding yourselves! Should not shepherds feed the sheep? You eat the fat, you clothe yourselves with the wool, you slaughter the fat ones, but you do not feed the sheep. The weak you have not strengthened, the sick you have not healed, the injured you have not bound up, the strayed you have not brought back, the lost you have not sought, and with force and harshness you have ruled them. So they were scattered, because there was no shepherd, and they became food for all the wild beasts. My sheep were scattered; they

wandered over all the mountains and on every high hill. My sheep were scattered over all the face of the earth, with none to search or seek for them.

## A Modern Example of "Teaching Shepherds"

In one of the meetings of the American Society for Church Growth, Karen Hurston reported on her book *Growing the World's Largest Church.*[8] Hurston is a seminary-trained, ordained pastor in the Assemblies of God. Her parents, missionaries for the Assemblies of God, recruited and trained Yonggi Cho, now the emeritus pastor of the largest congregation in the world, the Yoido Full Gospel Church in Seoul, South Korea. This community of believers started with six people meeting in a living room in 1958.[9] Today their membership approaches 1 million. Leaders from many denominations have gone to Seoul to learn the secret of this amazing growth.

Some of these visiting American pastors have noticed that this congregation in Seoul is part of the modern charismatic movement. They have such practices as speaking in tongues, miraculous healing and exorcism. Some of the American pastors have brought this charismatic influence back to mainline Protestant denominations. Most of the churches that tried this split and did not grow.

Other church leaders from America noticed the "cell groups" that are a vital part of this church. They brought back to America the cell-group approach. They tried to transition assembly-oriented churches and turn them into cell-group churches. But they split most of these churches, and they did not grow.

In her report to the American Society for Church Growth, Hurston said that most American church leaders have ignored the real key to the success and rapid growth of this church in Korea. That church has several hundred seminary-trained, full-time, church-supported pastors; as of December 2011 they had close to 700.[10] All of these pastors, from Cho on down the list, spend from one-third to one-half of their time counseling and teaching the members one person or one family at a time.

Their pastoral visits are very focused. They start with a few questions such as "How is your prayer life?" or "How is your family life?" "In what ministries are you involved?" Based on the answers to these questions, they have a few brief Bible lessons prepared and ready for delivery. But then they get down to some serious praying – highly personal and focused on the immediate needs of the individual or family. One of these pastoral visits usually lasts just half an hour.

When their seminary-trained, full-time, church-supported pastors make these visits, they do not go alone. They take with them the lay leader who works with the individual or family receiving the visit. Because this is how the lay leaders see the pastors relate to the members, they learn to relate to the members of their cell group in the same way.

Because that is the way the members see their pastors and their lay leaders communicating with them, it tends to become the way they communicate with other members of their cell group. That, I believe, is the kind of communication that imparts a blessing.

While I was listening to Karen Hurston's presentation, I was seated next to John Ellas, director of the Center for Church Growth in Houston, Texas. At that time, John was editor and publisher of the *Church Growth* magazine and the leading church-growth consultant among Churches of Christ. During a break in the meeting, I asked John if he thought that we should let Churches of Christ know about what we had just heard. He said that the elders would say, "Those were seminary-trained, ordained, full-time, church-supported pastors. The closest thing we have to that are our ministers. They need to do that kind of visiting." But the ministers would say, "Those were pastors, and it is the elders who need to do that kind of visiting." I told John I thought we should go ahead and tell Churches of Christ about what we had heard because elders and ministers should both be doing that kind of visiting!

## Conclusion

Many of the former members who responded to the "Why I Left Churches of Christ" survey might still be members if they had experienced the kind of interpersonal relationships that Christians need to have. Some may have been lost, at least in part, because of neglect by others. But a lesson church leaders need to learn is that relationships must not be neglected.

Far too many people experience church as a place they go. In that place, people come together as strangers and leave as strangers. Their lives never really touch. Someone's heart might be breaking, but the person seated next to him or her on the pew never knows about the other's suffering. A large worship assembly is not a good context for interpersonal bonding. I heard about someone who tried an experiment. He stood in the vestibule of a church building following a worship assembly. He greeted other church members when they left the auditorium. When they said, "How are you?" he replied "I am feeling terrible. I am so depressed that I have been thinking about killing myself." But when he said that, most of the people said, "That's great! See you at church next Sunday." The vestibule of a church building is probably not the best place for meaningful dialogue. It is more of a place for small talk. And small talk is okay; sometimes it grows up and becomes authentic dialogue. But if what Wagner called the "church as celebration" is the only level at which people experience church, they probably will never really be assimilated. That is why many people who "place membership" are never really "identified with the congregation."

It is hard to be invisible in a small congregation. But a large congregation that is successful will function as a collection of small congregation-like groups: Bible classes, fellowship groups, ministry groups, etc. Churches, whether large or small, need to correct the problem of letting people slip through the cracks. Some churches bring many people in through the "front door" but let them slip out the back door. It is time to close that back door.

Chapter **6**

# Those Who Did Not Fit In

In the responses to the survey of former members who have left Churches of Christ, one of the recurring themes has been that some people "just did not fit in." At least 10 listed this as their main reason for leaving. At least 20 others listed a different main reason for leaving Churches of Christ but at least mentioned in passing that they were never able to fit into the congregation. The following was typical of these observations.

> My husband and I attended a local congregation of the Churches of Christ for several years.[1] The members of this church seemed to be very friendly with one another, but they did not seem to pay much attention to newcomers. We tried to make friends, but the friendship circles were almost like cliques that did not need or want any outsiders. I had taught a Sunday school class at our former church home, and I offered to teach at this church – but never had the opportunity. My husband was a deacon at the church we attended before moving. He volunteered to help in several ministry areas, but his offers were ignored. Another newcomer (who also

> left Churches of Christ) said that in this congregation people were not even called on to lead a prayer until they had been in the church for five generations. That was probably an exaggeration, but just a few men ever led prayers in the assembly. Just a few served at the Lord's Supper. There were only two or three men who ever led the singing.
>
> Eventually we became discouraged and started looking around for another church home. There were no other congregations of the Churches of Christ in the town where we now live or within reasonable driving distance from our home. But we found a non-denominational community church that readily welcomed us, helped us get acquainted, put us to work and really assimilated us into the fellowship. We are satisfied with where we are now. We certainly feel closer to God now than we did before we left the Church of Christ in this community.

If we could talk to the members of the congregation this woman and her husband left, we might get a very different picture. It certainly is not my intention to put all the blame on the people in that church. But we asked former members to tell us why they left, and I believe that we should listen with an open mind to what they said. It might help us to look at things from the perspective of others.

No two people are identical. We like some people more than others. They have characteristics that appeal to us. We are comfortable around them. They are more likely to become our close personal friends. In much the same way, no two congregations are exactly alike. Personality differences may explain why some people fit in to one congregation but not into another. That, at least, is an idea that I would like to explore in this chapter.

If you think that I am using these comments by former members as an excuse to discuss the personality of a congregation, you are probably correct. I would ask, however, that you at least consider the possibility that personality may be a factor in why some people are attracted to one congregation and not to another and why some people stay in a congregations but others leave because they just do not fit in. I do not think that it should be that way, but I am fully persuaded that all too often it is.

## The Concept of a Group Personality

People who accept a naturalistic world view do not even believe that individuals have personalities, much less that there is any such thing as a "group personality." They believe that the only things that are real are physical things that can be weighed and measured – things that can be observed with the physical senses. Such concepts as "personality," "mind" and "selfhood" are too abstract for them.

When I was studying for a degree in psychology at the University of Houston, I took a course called "Emotion and Motivation." I thought that such a course might be valuable for a preacher. But on the first day of class, I told the professor that the bookstore had the wrong textbook. It was a book on brain physiology. But he explained that the bookstore had not made a mistake. That was the textbook he had adopted for that class. I never will forget his opening remarks in the class. "Emotion is nothing more than electro-chemical discharge from the brainstem reticular formation, and Motivation is nothing more than the interaction of that electro-chemical discharge at the upper cerebral cortex." We had a fascinating class in which I learned a great deal about the brain, but I do not think that I learned anything about emotion or motivation. That kind of reductionism worked well in the natural and physical sciences, but in my opinion it does not work at all well in the study of people. It certainly does not work well in the study of groups.

My guess is that the kind of people who would read a book such as this would not have any trouble believing that the personality of an individual is real. Some, however, may doubt that there really is such a thing as a group personality. But if you have been a member of more than one congregation, you probably have noticed that no two congregations are exactly alike. Each congregation has its own unique personality.

I find the concept of a group personality to be useful for studying the dynamics of a congregation. Consider, for example, the contrast between the first-century church in Jerusalem and the church in Syrian Antioch. Several years this side of Pentecost, the Jerusalem church was still very Jewish. At first they were very reluctant to believe that Gentiles could become Christians (Acts 10:1–11:18).

Later some of them insisted that Gentile converts had to be circumcised and keep the Law of Moses (15:1). Even after several more years, thousands of the Christians in Jerusalem were still "zealous for the law" (21:20). Some of them were still participating in the ceremonial purification rites at the temple (vv. 23-24). In Syrian Antioch, however, Gentiles were always welcomed into the church. Note that this first integrated church is where the disciples, for the first time, were called "Christians" (11:26).

As another example, consider the letters Jesus sent by way of John to the "Seven Churches" of Asia (Revelation 2:1–3:22). Each church had unique characteristics. The church in Ephesus had many good characteristics. They were commended for their hard work and perseverance. They were also commended for their refusal to tolerate false teachers. But they were condemned for having forsaken their first love (2:4). This church, by then at least 30 years old, had lost its original zeal. The church in Smyrna had been persecuted but was urged to remain faithful (vv. 9-10). The church in Philadelphia was the only other one of these seven churches that received no condemnation (3:7-12). The churches in Pergamum (2:14-16) and Thyatira (vv. 20-23) were both condemned because they tolerated false teachers. Although the church in Sardis had a faithful few, their group profile was one of a church that had a reputation of being alive when really they were dead spiritually (3:1). And the church in Laodicea became a synonym for a "lukewarm" church (vv. 15-16).

A congregation should welcome anyone who wants to be a part of that church. In Revelation 22:17 John wrote, "The Spirit and the Bride say, 'Come.' And let the one who hears say, 'Come.' And let the one who is thirsty come; let the one who desires take the water of life without price." I believe that the sentiment of the children's song is right: "Jesus loves the little children; all the children of the world. Red and yellow, black and white; they are precious in his sight. Jesus loves the little children of the world." There is only one race: the human race. All other distinctions are artificial and arbitrary.

In the early years of my ministry, I opposed racial segregation so strongly that I doubted that the so-called "Black church" should exist. All of the Blacks should be a part of my predominately white church.

But unconsciously, I assumed that it would still be "my" kind of church. The preaching would be in the style of the dominant white culture, not the melodic delivery of the African storyteller. The songs we would sing would reflect Western musical forms, not the African-American style of the old spirituals.

Donald McGavran, father of the modern Church Growth Movement, was the one who persuaded me that "Men like to become Christians without crossing racial, linguistic or class barriers." [2] This is McGavran's "homogeneous unit principle" that has often been misunderstood. McGavran's critics accused him of defending segregation. When I went to Fuller Seminary for the organizational meetings of the American Society for Church Growth[3] and got to meet McGavran, I came to the conclusion that there was not a bigoted bone in that little man's body. He just wanted to reach as many people as possible with the gospel of Jesus Christ. He was convinced that some segments of the population in America will not be reached in a white mainstream culture congregation.

I now believe that McGavran was right. However, I also believe that a congregation should welcome anyone who wants to be a part of that church regardless of racial/ethnic identity, socio-economic status or even personality type. In America, at least for now, there may be a need for churches in which people speak Spanish or some Asian language. Even after people learn English, their prayer language may continue to be the language they first learned. Most people will not be persuaded to become Christians except in their "heart language."

## The Need for Diversity in the Church

The church is a body with many different members that perform many different functions in many different ways (1 Corinthians 12). The church must have this kind of diversity to survive. A body must be able to change, grow and adapt itself to its environment to survive. A congregation needs members with as many different gifts as possible.

In Romans 12:4-6, Paul wrote, "For as in one body we have many members, and the members do not all have the same function, so we, though many, are one body in Christ, and individually members one of another. Having gifts that differ according to the grace given to us, let us use them." What follows in the rest of Romans 12 is a list of different gifts. In this passage, the emphasis seems to be on "service gifts" – natural endowments especially sanctified when we become Christians and used for the good of the whole body.

In 1 Corinthians 12:4-7, Paul wrote, "Now there are varieties of gifts, but the same Spirit; and there are varieties of service, but the same Lord; and there are varieties of activities, but it is the same God who empowers them all in everyone. To each is given the manifestation of the Spirit for the common good." What follows through the rest of 1 Corinthians 12 seems to be an emphasis on "sign gifts" – supernatural powers given to various first-century Christians to confirm the Word. But the principle is still the same; we do not all have the same gifts.

Peter wrote, "Each one should use whatever gifts he has received to serve others, faithfully administering God's grace in its various forms" (1 Peter 4:10 NIV1984). And in the verse 11, Peter mentions those who speak and those who serve – presumably preachers and deacons. But we are not all supposed to be preachers, and we are not all supposed to be deacons.

James 3:1 warns, "Not many of you should become teachers, my brothers, for you know that we who teach will be judged with greater strictness." Some people do not have the gift of teaching. Have you ever been in a class with a teacher who did not have the gift of teaching and took an entire semester to prove it?

For maximum effectiveness, a church needs to have members with as many different gifts as possible. That is especially true in regard to the personality differences called "psychological types." Carefully controlled scientific experiments have demonstrated that homogeneous groups function better for simple repetitive tasks. Heterogeneous groups, however, function much better when the tasks are more complicated. In a heterogeneous group, communication will be more of a challenge. It may take longer to make decisions, but the quality of the decisions will be much better. Working effectively as a congregation does not consist of simple repetitive tasks. Working effectively together is about as complicated a task as one can find.

## Studying Characteristics of a Congregation

When I have conducted congregational assessments, I have compared demographics in the church with those in the community. I start with data on a congregation's "ministry area." Then I have church leaders provide similar demographic data on the congregation. If members of a congregation are 99 percent White/Anglo, but their community is 10 percent Black and 15 percent Hispanic, I would conclude that racial/ethnic identity has played a role in who comes and who stays in that church. Sometimes the age distribution in the congregation shows far more older members and fewer younger members than what one would expect based on the age distribution in the community. For the age group comparison one simply takes the percentage of an age group in the church and divides that by the percentage of the same age group in the community. The result is a ratio index. If that index is 1.00, the church matches the community perfectly in that age group. If the index is 2.00, there are twice as many church members in that age group as what one would expect on the basis of the percentage of that age group in the community. If the index is 0.50, then the church has only half as many members in that age group as what one would expect based on the percentage of that age group in the community.

The same approach is used to study the personality of a congregation. For that purpose, I use the most popular personality inventory in the history of psychology: The Myers-Briggs Type Indicator. The rest of this chapter explains the method that I use to identify the personality of a congregation. If you already understand that there is such a thing as a "group personality" and if you are turned off by psychological jargon, you might want to skip the rest of this chapter. It may appear to be more than you ever wanted to know or cared to ask about Yeakley's method for identifying the personality of a congregation. However, I think that this material is important enough to include in this book.

## Carl Jung's Theory of Psychological Types

The research I have done on the personality of congregations has been based on Carl G. Jung's theory of Psychological Types. A brief introduction to that theory is essential at this point in the discussion.[4]

Jung observed that there are two mental processes that are fundamental: perception and judgment. All people must take in information and make decisions about what they perceive. But Jung came to the conclusion that there are two opposite ways of perceiving that are equally valuable. He called these "Sensing" and "Intuition." Sensing perception focuses on details while Intuition focuses more on patterns and meanings. Sensing perception trusts historical precedents while Intuition is guided more by a vision of what could be in the future. Healthy mature adults use both Sensing and Intuition but not with equal competence, confidence and conscious control. Jung believed that people are born with a preference for one of these two ways of perceiving.

Jung also believed that there are two ways of judging that are opposite but equally valuable. The English translation of *Psychological Types* called these "Thinking" and "Feeling." These terms, however, have often been misunderstood. If people have a preference for Thinking judgment it does not mean that they have no heart. It just means that they prefer to be as objective as possible in making their judgments. They try to be logical. Those who have a preference for Feeling judgment prefer to make decisions in a more subjective way. They must, at least vicariously, get in the middle of the situation and see how their values and the values of others are involved. "Feeling," for Jung, does not mean emotionality. There are times when all of us need to use Thinking judgment and other times when Feeling judgment is required. But Jung believed that people are born with a preference for either Thinking or Feeling judgment.

The concept of "Preferences" is central in Jung's theory of psychological types. Psychologists have developed many personality inventories that measure how much or how little of various traits people have. Scores on a trait instrument generally fall along the familiar line of a bell-shaped curve. Having too much or too little of a trait such as Dominance, for example, is considered abnormal and unhealthy. The desirable place to score is around the middle of the bell curve.

Jung did not think that way. He was more impressed by natural sciences such as botany or zoology that classified plants and animals with less concern for measurement. Jung's theory of psychological types is a theory of dichotomies: a preference for one or the other of the two ways of perceiving and the two ways of judging.

Sign your name in the way you usually do and then put the pen in the other hand and sign your name again. You will probably find that your signature made with your non-dominant hand looks more primitive. It probably took you longer and required more conscious effort to write your name with your non-dominant hand. The point, however, is that you were able to use both hands – just not with equal skill. That is the way it is with preferences for one or the other ways of perceiving and the ways of judging. The important issue in Psychological type theory is to correctly identify the preferences of individuals and not to measure how much or how little of some trait they have.

Jung devoted more than half of his book *Psychological Types* to a discussion of another dichotomy: two opposite but equally valuable attitudes that he called "Extraversion" and "Introversion." These are directions that people prefer to take for finding and using their mental energy. Those with a preference for extraversion are energized by the external world – especially by interactions with other people. Introverts, on the other hand, get their energy by "going inside" to meditate and reflect. They do their best work alone.

Extraverts and Introverts differ in how they prefer to use their favorite mental function (Sensing, Intuition, Thinking and Feeling). Extraverts prefer to use their most fully developed and most trusted mental function for dealing with the external world. What you see when you talk to an Extravert, therefore, is the dominant function – the function that is in control of their personality. Introverts, on the other hand, prefer to use their favorite mental function internally for reflection and meditation. They prefer to use an auxiliary function for dealing with the external world. Extraverts are more likely to answer questions quickly, but they may get it wrong and later change their minds. Introverts have to "get it in" before they can "get it out." It takes them longer to answer a question, but they are less likely to change their mind later.

Jung briefly mentioned one other dichotomy: the difference between two orientations to the external world. Some people prefer to extravert a perceiving function (Sensing or Intuition). They may take longer to make a decision because they always want to take in more information.

People who prefer to deal with the external world through a judging function (Thinking or Feeling) are motivated to make decisions quickly, even when the data are incomplete.

Jung believed that the four mental functions are like four different languages. The function that is extraverted is the Primary communication style. The function that is normally used internally for reflection and meditation is a Secondary communication style. The two other functions, the Tertiary and the Least-Preferred, are like languages that are seldom used. Healthy mature people use all four communication styles when needed, but they have an order of preference in which the four styles are used.

## The Myers-Briggs Type Indicator (MBTI)

Results of the Myers-Briggs Type Indicator[5] should help identify a person's preferences for one or the other of four dichotomies:

Extraversion (E) or Introversion (I)
Sensing (S) or Intuition (N)[6]
Thinking (T) or Feeling (F)
Judging (J) or Perceiving (P)

No two people are exactly alike, and no inventory is adequate to explain the human personality. A wide margin of error exists around the results of any personality inventory. That being the case, it is not at all unusual that roughly one-fourth of the people who take the MBTI disagree with their results as they learn more about their psychological type. Usually they disagree with the results on only one of the four dichotomies, and usually that one was a dichotomy on which the MBTI did not give a clear reading. When people take the MBTI, they generally receive a report form that indicates their preferences on the four dichotomies and also shows how clearly that preference was indicated. These are not numbers that show how much or how little of some trait a person has. They just show how much confidence a person should have that his or her true preference has been indicated.

When I conduct research on the "group personality" of a congregation, the unit of analysis is the MBTI type table as seen in Table 6.1. This table is a four-by-four matrix with 16 types. The eight types with preferences for Introversion (I) are listed in the two top rows, and the eight types that prefer Extraversion (E) are in the two bottom rows. The eight Sensing types (S) are listed in the two columns on the left while the eight types that prefer Intuition (N) are in the two columns on the right. The eight Thinking types (T) are listed in the columns on the far right and far left sides of the type table with the eight Feeling types (F) listed in the two middle columns. Finally, the eight types that prefer to deal with the external world through a Judging (J) function (Thinking or Feeling) are listed in the top and bottom rows with the eight types that prefer a perceiving (P) function (Sensing or Intuition) are listed in the two middle rows.

Because one-fourth of the people who take the MBTI end up changing their understanding of their true type, the type table distribution is not exact. However, it is likely that changes will be random, and the overall type table distribution will remain the same. The purpose of these studies is to identify the personality of the congregation, not of any one individual.

## Table 6.1

Distribution of the 16 MBTI Types
in the General Population

| ISTJ | | ISFJ | | INFJ | | INTJ | |
|---|---|---|---|---|---|---|---|
| males | females | males | females | males | females | males | females |
| 16.4% | 6.9% | 8.1% | 19.4% | 1.3% | 1.6% | 3.3% | 0.8% |
| **ISTP** | | **ISFP** | | **INFP** | | **INTP** | |
| males | females | males | females | males | females | males | females |
| 8.5% | 2.4% | 7.6% | 9.9% | 4.1% | 4.6% | 4.8% | 1.8% |
| **ESTP** | | **ESFP** | | **ENFP** | | **ENTP** | |
| males | females | males | females | males | females | males | females |
| 5.6% | 3.0% | 6.9% | 10.1% | 6.4% | 9.7% | 4.0% | 2.4% |
| **ESTJ** | | **ESFJ** | | **ENFJ** | | **ENTJ** | |
| males | females | males | females | males | females | males | females |
| 11.2% | 6.3% | 7.5% | 16.9% | 1.6% | 3.3% | 2.7% | 0.9% |

Table 6.1 shows the distribution of the 16 MBTI types in the general population.[7] Notice that in most type table studies, data on males and females are reported separately. The reason for this is that 56.5 percent of males prefer Thinking judgment while 75.5 percent of females prefer Feeling judgment (see Table 6.2). That distinction is lost when male and female data are combined.

From what the New Testament says about diversity of gifts in the church, I would conclude that a congregation should welcome and assimilate all kinds of people. If personality has not been a factor in who comes and who stays, I would expect to see a distribution of the 16 MBTI types that is relatively close to the population norms as shown in Table 6.1. The statistic that is used in this kind of study is called a "Self Selection Ratio Index" (SSR). It is calculated in the same way as a ratio index in demographic comparisons – by taking the percentage of church members who have one of the 16 MBTI types and dividing it by the percentage of that type in the general population.

## Summary by Preferences

In a study of a congregation, there will be 16 SSRs for males and 16 more for females. It is often hard to detect a pattern in such study with 32 separate SSRs. Patterns are more likely to be noticed in summaries. Table 6.2, for example, shows the summary by preferences on the four dichotomies.

### Table 6.2

Summary by Preferences

| Extraversion | | | Introversion |
|---|---|---|---|
| males | 45.9% | males | 54.1% |
| females | 52.5% | females | 47.5% |
| Sensing | | | Intuition |
| males | 71.7% | males | 28.3% |
| females | 74.9% | females | 25.1% |
| Thinking | | | Feeling |
| males | 56.5% | males | 43.5% |
| females | 24.5% | females | 75.5% |
| Judging | | | Perceiving |
| males | 52.0% | males | 48.0% |
| females | 56.2% | females | 43.8% |

Using a summary by preferences for the whole group and not just the 16 MBTI types, in a large random sample of males, we would expect the ISTJ description to come closest to a good fit with the group (male preferences: 54.1% introversion, 71.7% sensing, 56.5% thinking and

52.0% judging). In a large random sample of females, we would expect the ESFJ description to be the best fit (female preferences: 52.5% extraversion, 74.9% sensing, 75.5% feeling and 56.2% judging). If the distribution in a congregation is significantly different from this, that pattern would show which type was attracted to that church and which type just did not fit.

My father, Flavil R. Yeakley Sr., was known as a "troubleshooter" in ministry. He preached for several congregations that were badly divided when he arrived. Those churches did not always resolve their conflicts, but they at least learned to manage them. One of the things my father taught me is that most church splits are because of personalities. They may find some doctrinal argument to justify the split, but the real reason for the division was that people with different personalities were unable to work together. An MBTI profile of a divided congregation is one way of demonstrating that their differences are more because of personalities than doctrine.

When I wrote *Why Churches Grow*, I mentioned a study I did in a large sample of congregations. The pulpit ministers in these congregations took the MBTI. Adult members who had affiliated with that congregation during the tenure of that preacher – either by adult conversion or by transfer of membership – also took the MBTI. The results showed that Thinker-type preachers were attracting Thinker-type members but fewer Feeler-type members, and the church became more and more inbred.

At first I blamed the preachers for building churches around their own personalities. But then I started doing congregational assessments, and I found that the churches were that way before the preachers ever came. A Thinker-type church selects a Thinker-type preacher. He attracts more Thinker-type members. And the church becomes more and more inbred.

In one city I did congregational assessments for three different churches. One had a big over-representation of Thinkers and an under-representation of Feelers. A few miles away there was a Feeler-type church with very few Thinkers. The Thinker church did not like the Feeler church. They thought that the Feelers were a bunch of "liberals." The Feeler church did not like the Thinker church. They thought that the Thinkers were a bunch of "narrow-minded legalists." An inner-city ministry with many Sensing-type members thought that those other churches ought to stop fighting each other and do something practical like helping to feed the hungry and provide shelter for the homeless.

**Table 6.3**

Summary by Communication Style Preferences

| | |
|---|---|
| **Sensing** | |
| males | 28.6% |
| females | 25.3% |
| **Intuition** | |
| males | 19.4% |
| females | 18.5% |
| **Thinking** | |
| males | 33.6% |
| females | 15.0% |
| **Feeling** | |
| males | 18.5% |
| females | 41.2% |

## Summary by Communication Style Preferences

Table 6.3 shows the summary by Communication Style Preferences. That is the kind of analysis that is most interesting to me. I took the MBTI for the first time in 1969 when I was taking a Psychological Testing class at the University of Houston. I take the MBTI again every time a new form is published, and I have always come out as INTJ. What that means in terms of communication styles is that I talk Thinker language most of the time, but my dominant mental function is Intuition. That is how I talk to myself, meditate and reflect. I started preaching in 1950 when I was 16 years old and a sophomore in high school. I was on the debate team at the high school in Ardmore, Okla. Looking back I can see that most of my sermons back then sounded like the first affirmative address in a debate. That may sound bad, but it is not as bad as some preachers I know whose sermons still sound like the last negative rebuttal.

I was at least 20 years old before I learned to take my dominant introverted intuition and get it out where others could see it. For several years I preached what I thought were some of the most eloquent sermons the world has ever heard on "The Meaning of Human Existence and Our Place in the Universe," "The Nature of God," "What Is Sin?" and similar topics. Those sermons went over like lead balloons. They fell flat. The engineers, mechanics, accountants and farmers in my audiences just were not interested. Some of them said, "Give us something practical – something to get us through the week." I replied, "There is nothing as practical as a good theory." I still believe that to be true, but those people were not convinced.

I was more than 30 years old before I learned to preach in my tertiary communication style, Feeling. Although I have appeared as a speaker on lectureships and workshops throughout the nation, I have never been invited to be the "closer." That assignment calls for someone who is really good at preaching in Feeler language.

I was 40 years old before I learned to preach in Sensing style – simple "how-to" sermons. That is still not what I do best. But when I was asked to serve as the treasurer of the Association for Psychological Type, my wife laughed. She balances our checkbook. Once a year I get everything together for the CPA so I have a good grasp of the big picture, but my wife tends to the details. Fortunately, APT had accountants and clerical help who tended to those details. My focus was on strategic planning. That is what I did for 10 years as treasurer, president-elect and then president.

I was around 40 years old when I started doing statistical research on patterns of growth and decline among Churches of Christ in the United States. If I am known for anything at all outside my immediate family, it is probably for the statistical studies and survey research that I have done. That kind of work calls for a Sensing function with a clear emphasis on details. But I am sure I could not have done that kind of work before the age of 40. Even today when I attend meetings of the Association of Statisticians of American Religious Bodies, I notice that I am not like those official denominational statisticians. They enjoy doing statistics. I use my Sensing function to do statistics, but only in the service of my dominant introverted Intuition. I have a vision, a dream and a higher purpose of helping churches improve. That is what keeps me going. But I could never be a full-time statistician. I do not do statistics for the fun of it.

When I have taught preaching classes, I have had my students take the MBTI so that they know their personal preferences. But then I urge them to learn how to "preach to the whole church" – how to communicate in all four of these languages. That is one of the reasons that I favor narrative preaching that tells the simple story of Jesus. Stories have power. A preacher can preach the same sermon or at least preach on the same text two times in a row, and few people will notice it. But if a preacher uses the same illustration he used a year or two ago, everyone remembers. The four Gospels are narrative sermons telling the story of Jesus.

Incidentally, I am persuaded that Matthew wrote in Thinker communication style. He uses a very logical structure showing what the prophets said the Messiah would do, then showing that this is what Jesus did with the conclusion that Jesus is the Messiah. Matthew includes much of what Jesus said. It is the longest of the four Gospels. Mark, on the other hand, is the shortest. It is action-oriented with very little of what Jesus said and much of what he did. I believe that Mark wrote in Sensing communication style. John is the Gospel that is easiest to identify in regard to communication style. Intuition is the communication style one sees throughout John. He steps back from the synoptic and gives us the rest of the story – the big picture about some things the others left out. Luke is probably the most eloquent Greek and the best mix of all four communication styles. But in Luke more than in the others we see what Jesus valued. We see his respect for the role of women. We see his compassion for the poor. Perhaps by default, I would say that Luke wrote in Feeler communication style.

Jung was right when he said that Sensing, Intuition, Thinking and Feeling are like four different languages. Furthermore, Isabel Myers was right when she used the title *Gifts Differing* for her explanation of the MBTI. The language, of course, comes from the King James Version of Romans 6:6, "Having then gifts differing according to the grace that is given to us … ." All 16 of the MBTI types show people with different gifts. Churches need all of these gifts, not just half of them.

Psychological type differences are reflected in different prayer styles. One way I learned this was in early Saturday morning prayer meetings with preachers and elders. Those group prayer sessions were like mountain peak experiences for the extraverts in the group. I wondered what was wrong with me for preferring to pray alone. Have you ever been in a prayer group with extraverts who make "comments" while you are trying to pray? They keep saying things like, "Amen," "Yes Lord," or just "Uh-huh." I resisted my natural inclinations to tell the extraverts, "Hush! I am trying to talk to God over here." Eventually I learned that it is okay for the extraverts to make "comments" when they pray, and it is okay for me to avoid such "distractions."

## Table 6.4

Summary by Quadrants

| | |
|---|---|
| **IS** | |
| males | 40.5% |
| females | 38.6% |
| **ES** | |
| males | 31.2% |
| females | 36.3% |
| **EN** | |
| males | 14.7% |
| females | 16.3% |
| **IN** | |
| males | 13.5% |
| females | 8.9% |

## Summary by Quadrants

There are many other ways of combining groups of four in an MBTI type table. Each has its personal particular application. I want to discuss one more before leaving this subject. Table 6.4 shows the summary by quadrants. In his book *People Types and Tiger Stripes*, Gordon D. Lawrence suggests that students in the four quadrants of the type table (IS, ES, EN, and IN) do their best work in different situations.[8] Lawrence and several others have suggested that people in these four quadrants have different ways of dealing with change. In a two-page handout on "Finding and Following Your Spiritual Path," Earl Paige suggested different slogans appropriate for each quadrant.[9] Moving through the four quadrants in counter-clockwise direction, these slogans would be:

| | |
|---|---|
| **IS** | "Keep It!" |
| **ES** | "Just Do It!" |
| **EN** | "Change It!" |
| **IN** | "Think about it in a different way!" |

Personally, I think that this is an over-simplification. However, in the more than 100 congregations where I have done MBTI studies, most of the preachers have been in the EN quadrant and have been advocates of change. A large majority of the elders have been in the IS or ES quadrants and have been much less favorable to change.

Several years ago we had a leadership seminar at Harding University that was attended by more than 100 elders and preachers. They all took my self-scorable version of the MBTI.[10] All of the preachers were in the EN quadrant. A majority of the elders were in the IS quadrant. A few were in the ES quadrant. Only one elder was in the EN quadrant, and he was both a preacher and an elder. Some of the conflict over change could be managed better if those involved understood these natural and healthy differences in how people prefer to use their perception and their judgment.

The quadrants of the MBTI type table provide some useful information about how groups are likely to respond to change. But it is not as simple as that sounds. The biggest difference regarding change is the Sensing-Intuition dichotomy. Sensing types tend to be like Patrick Henry who said in 1775, "I have but one lamp by which my feet are guided; and that is the lamp of experience." Sensing types make up more than 70 percent of the population. They are more likely to accept change if it is presented as "a continuation of what already exists and just needs to be improved." If the change sounds like something totally new, they are likely to view it negatively. Because those who prefer Intuition focus more on future possibilities, they tend to be advocates of change. These are sub-divided into the EN group that includes people who tend to favor any change and the IN group that wants a more fundamental change in the way people view things.

It is beyond the scope of this book to continue this discussion of psychological-type theory much longer. But I would not want to end this discussion of organizational change without pointing readers to a valuable resource: *Introduction to Type and Teams* by Elizabeth Hirsh, Katherine W. Hirsh and Sandra Krebs Hirsh.[11] This 52-page booklet provides a wealth of information – including how each of the 16 types is likely to react to organizational change.

## Conclusion

A church needs all of the gifts, not just half of them. A church needs to welcome and assimilate all kinds of people. It is not wrong for a congregation to have a unique personality. What is wrong is for a church to become an inbred clique. What is even worse is for a church to take on characteristics of a cult.

In 1985 I did a different kind of MBTI study in the Boston Church of Christ. That congregation was, at that time, the *de facto* headquarters for a discipling movement that had started at the Crossroads Church of Christ in Gainesville, Fla. In 1994 that movement took on the name "International Churches of Christ" and asked not to be listed with other Churches of Christ in almanacs and yearbooks.

Critics had charged that this movement put unnatural and unhealthy pressure on people to change and conform in ways that had nothing to do with Christianity. They were charged with making clones out of their converts. Leaders of that movement had always denied that charge.

Early in 1985, one of the elders of the Boston Church of Christ asked the president of Abilene Christian University to send someone to Boston to document the amazing story of rapid growth in that church. At that time I was working as a Researcher in Residence at ACU. I was the one sent to Boston. At that time I was working on the development of what eventually became the Form G Self-Scorable version of the MBTI. I had the publisher's permission to make copies of my experimental "Form Y" and use it in research.

More than 900 members of the Boston Church of Christ took the MBTI three times with different instructions. First, they were told to answer the questions the way they thought, felt and acted at that present time. Then, they were told to answer the questions the way they would have before they became members of that church. Finally, they were told to answer the questions the way they thought they would answer them after five more years of "discipling." They were told that there are no "right" or "wrong" answers and no "good" or "bad" outcomes. They were also told that there was no reason for changing their responses from the "past" to the "present" and on to the "future" perceptions of themselves.

I had previously used that "past/present/future" methodology in MBTI studies of Churches of Christ not identified with the discipling movement and with five mainline denominations: Baptist, Methodist, Catholic, Lutheran and Presbyterian. The results in these studies showed minor variations, but no significant changes in the type table distribution. Then we tested six manipulative cult-like sects: the Church of Scientology, Hare Krishna, Maranatha, Children of God, Unification Church ("Moonies"), and the Way International. In each of these groups, there were dramatic changes from the "past" to the "present" and on to the "future" perceptions of self. Furthermore, in each case there was a clear convergence in a single type.

My wife, Maydell Yeakley, and a few of her friends spent the next few months hand-scoring those MBTI results from Boston. The pattern that finally emerged was exactly what I had observed in the six cult-like manipulative sects. There were highly significant changes in the type table distributions, and there was a clear convergence in a single type: ESFJ. There is nothing wrong with being an ESFJ. They are beautiful people. I have been married to an ESFJ since June 1, 1954. As I already mentioned, ISTJ and ESFJ are the two types most likely to be modal types in a congregation. What is wrong is to pressure people to become clones of a group leader or a group norm. Healthy growth and development occurs within type, not by changing from one type to another. Pressure to conform in ways that have nothing to do with Christianity can damage people emotionally and spiritually.[12]

Psychological type does not explain everything. It may not explain why some of these former members of the Churches of Christ left because they "just did not fit in." But I thought that this possible explanation would be worth considering.

Chapter 7

# Divorce and Remarriage Issues

Several of those who responded to the "Why I Left Churches of Christ" survey listed divorce and remarriage issues as reasons. Some of these listed no other reasons. But before discussing what they said, I need to remind you that this was not a random sample. If we could contact every former member and asked why each left, a few would probably say something similar to what you will read in this chapter. This survey, however, does not provide an estimate of how many would mention divorce and remarriage issues. But there is something far more important than the limitations of this study that must be understood. Even if a significant number of members are leaving because of these issues that would not justify changing doctrines or practices. We must never do theology by opinion poll or popular vote. Hearing from these people about why they left could at least be an occasion for a serious review of what the Bible teaches on these matters.

It is not my purpose in this chapter to discuss my personal views on these issues. I am not trying to persuade others to see things as I do. That would distract from the purpose of this book. What I am trying to do here is to report what these former members of the Churches of Christ said about why they left.

One of the things I have learned about divorce and remarriage issues is that equally qualified and equally devout Bible scholars differ in their conclusions. I am a student of Restoration Movement history. My master's thesis at the University of Houston was a study of how rhetorical strategies used by movement leaders help to explain why the Stone-Campbell Restoration Movement divided on some issues but managed to differ without dividing on other issues.[1] My conclusion on this matter was that this movement is too divided to split because of these related issues. Movements are far more likely to divide when two clearly defined groups are on opposite sides of an issue. In the history of the Stone-Campbell Restoration Movement, a separation into conflicting groups has been much more likely when each side was represented by well-known leaders, different journals or different schools. Tolerating a diversity of viewpoints has been more likely when more than two views were being expressed. Such a tolerance for diversity, however, is not always healthy – not when it is bought at the price of benign neglect and studied silence. An open and honest dialogue is much healthier. Such a dialogue may not result in a consensus acceptable to all involved. It could, however, be an important step in that direction. I offer these reflections in the hope that they may be a stimulus to such a dialogue.

I believe that we should approach this study with great humility. We should recognize that we are not perfect in our understanding of God's will. We should be willing to consider alternative interpretations with open minds. But what we decide to teach and practice must be guided by Scripture. In that spirit I offer my personal reflections on the explanations that some gave concerning why they left the Churches of Christ.

## "No Grounds for Divorce"

Two who responded to this survey had been members of congregations where the preachers taught that the marriage relationship can be broken only by death. Divorce was never allowed.

> My husband had numerous affairs. Each time when I caught him, he said that he was sorry and that if I would forgive him, he would never do it again. But each time he did it again. I lost count of how many times he has been guilty of

> adultery. He broke our marriage vows so many times that it destroyed my trust. I was afraid that I would get some sexually transmitted disease that he caught from one of his sex partners and then passed on to me. I talked to our preacher about this and he said that I could leave my husband, but I could never marry anyone else. He said that in God's sight I would always be married to him. Eventually I got a divorce, but the church members all shunned me. That is why I left. I am now a member of a community church where I am accepted. In this church I met and married a fine Christian man. I would never go back to the Church of Christ because of what they teach on this matter.

This second response went into more detail about what the preacher in a congregation of the Churches of Christ taught on this subject.

> My first husband had his first affair just after we returned from our honeymoon, and many other affairs followed. I urged him to go with me for marriage counseling, but he refused. I went to our minister for guidance. He had me read Romans 7:2-3, "For the woman who has a husband is bound by law to her husband as long as he lives. But if the husband dies, she is released from the law of her husband. So then if, while her husband lives, she marries another man, she will be called an adulteress; but if her husband dies, she is free from that law, so that she is no adulteress, though she has married another man" (NKJV). Then he had me read Mark 10:11-12 where Jesus said, "Whoever divorces his wife and marries another commits adultery against her. And if a woman divorces her husband and marries another she commits adultery" (NKJV).
>
> I asked our minister about what Jesus said in the Sermon on the Mount in Matthew 5:31-32, "Furthermore it has been said, 'Whoever divorces his wife, let him give her a certificate of divorce.' But I say to you that whoever divorces his wife for any reason except sexual immorality causes her

> to commit adultery; and whoever marries a woman who is divorced commits adultery" (NKJV). He said that this does not mean that adultery is scriptural grounds for divorce. It just means that a man who divorces his wife because of her adultery does not cause her to become an adulteress since that is what she already is.

In my opinion, most Churches of Christ do not accept this "no grounds for divorce" doctrine. Most believe that the exception language in Matthew 5:31-32 authorizes divorce on the grounds of adultery. Most also believe that the innocent party in such a divorce is free to marry again. My best estimate is that fewer than 5 percent of people in Churches of Christ accept this "no divorce" doctrine. Although that doctrine is affirmed by Catholics, very few Protestants accept it.

Most members of the Churches of Christ believe that in Romans 7:2-3, Paul was not discussing marriage. He was using marriage as an illustration. His subject was how we are no longer under the Law of Moses. An argument by analogy uses the general rule, not any possible exceptions to that rule. And the argument based on Mark 10:11-12 ignores the larger context that begins in verse 2, "And Pharisees came up and in order to test him asked, 'Is it lawful for a man to divorce his wife?' " Those Pharisees were not really asking for information. They just wanted to trap Jesus. There is a parallel passage in Matthew 19:3-9 where Matthew includes some information not mentioned in Mark 10:2-12. Instead of the Pharisees asking, "Is it lawful for a man to divorce his wife?" the question in Matthew 19:3 was, "Is it lawful to divorce one's wife for any cause?"

Matthew seems to have been addressed primarily to a Jewish audience. Jewish readers would have known about the controversy between the schools of Shammai and Hillel on the interpretation of Deuteronomy 24:1-4. That is where Moses wrote,

> When a man takes a wife and marries her, if then she finds no favor in his eyes because he has found some indecency in her, and he writes her a certificate of divorce and puts it in her hand and sends her out of his house, and she departs out of his house, and if she goes and becomes another man's wife, and the latter man hates her and writes her a certificate

> of divorce and puts it in her hand and sends her out of his house, or if the latter man dies, who took her to be his wife, then her former husband, who sent her away, may not take her again to be his wife, after she has been defiled, for that is an abomination before the LORD. And you shall not bring sin upon the land that the LORD your God is giving you for an inheritance.

It is unclear how that second marriage "defiled" the woman. The reference may be to ceremonial uncleanness. It might be like the rule that a woman was not allowed to come to the tabernacle or later to the temple when she was having her period or that a man who had touched a dead body was ceremonially unclean. Some Bible scholars believe that the reference may be to the possibility that the woman might be pregnant carrying the second husband's child when she remarries the first husband. There could then be a question of paternity.

Shammai held that "some indecency in her" (Deuteronomy 24:1) referred to sexual immorality, and that would be the only acceptable grounds for divorce. Hillel focused on the part of the verse that said if the wife finds "no favor" in her husband's eyes (v. 1). He allowed a man to divorce his wife if she did anything that displeased him – even if she burned the food while preparing a meal.

It seems clear that Jesus did not agree with Hillel, but Jesus did not take sides in the debate between Shammai and Hillel. Instead he focused on the creation purposes of marriage. "Have you not read that he who created them from the beginning made them male and female, and said, 'Therefore a man shall leave his father and his mother and hold fast to his wife, and the two shall become one flesh'? So they are no longer two but one flesh. What therefore God has joined together, let not man separate." (Matthew 19:4-6).

Some people have understood the language of Matthew 19:6 and Mark 10:9, "What therefore God has joined together, let not man separate," to mean that marriage is indissoluble – that those God has joined together cannot be separated. But that is not what these passages say. People are told not to separate what God has joined together, but that does not mean that it cannot be done. In the Ten Commandments, people were told not to murder, commit adultery, steal, give false witness or covet. But that did not mean that they could not do these things – just that they were not supposed to do them.

Perhaps one of the reasons that Jesus did not enter into the debate between Shammai and Hillel was that both sides in this debate ignored the context of Deuteronomy 24:1-4. It is clear from this passage that Moses did not create divorce. Divorce already existed. Moses simply regulated one aspect of something that was already being done. What Moses prohibited was a divorced wife who had married a second husband going back to her first husband if her second husband divorced her or died. What was more important than interpreting Deuteronomy 24:1-4 was understanding the creation purposes of marriage. Both Shammai and Hillel seem to have developed doctrines about divorce that were not based on a theology of marriage. It seems to me that most of the recent books on the subjects of divorce and remarriage make that same mistake.

## "Adultery as the Only Grounds for Divorce"

From what I have seen, it would appear that more than half of the people in Churches of Christ believe that adultery is grounds for divorce and that is the only grounds acceptable to God. That view presented problems for some of the people who responded to the survey and explained why they left Churches of Christ. The following are some of the things they wrote:

> I was a battered wife of an alcoholic husband. About once a week he would come home drunk and beat me. Through the years I suffered a broken jaw, a broken nose, a broken arm and too many black eyes to count. Then when beating me was not enough, he started beating our children. That was more than I could stand. I took the children and went to a shelter home for battered women. As soon as I could, I divorced him. Our pastor said that it was probably necessary for me to leave my husband and get a divorce. But he said that in the sight of God I was still married to him since the divorce was not because of adultery. I could not understand why all the beatings that I and the children endured would

> not be as big an offense as having sex with a prostitute one time. That was why I left the Church of Christ.

Here is what another wrote:

> My wife became a drug addict, and it was not just "recreational" use of marijuana. She was injecting heroin. As far as I know, she never committed adultery. But things got so bad that she tried to sell our infant daughter to get the money she needed to feed her habit. That is why I divorced her. But the elders of our church told me that since there was no proof of adultery, I could never remarry. When I eventually did remarry, those elders said that I was "living in adultery." I had to leave that congregation or else be expelled. My second wife is a Pentecostal, and I joined her church.

Another response was quite different from the personal stories about divorce. This one had more to do with doctrines concerning remarriage.

> I was actively involved in personal evangelism. I learned how to use the Jule Miller filmstrips and Ivan Stewart's Open Bible Study method. Through the years I must have baptized at least a dozen people. But then I was studying with a couple in a mixed-up marital situation. Both of them had been married before. Both divorced their first marital partners for reasons other than adultery. Later they met, fell in love, and got married. They now have a happy family life with three children. When they decided to obey the gospel, the preacher and the elders of the church refused permission for me to baptize them because they were living in adultery. They said that they could not be baptized until they divorced each other and remarried their first mates or else took a vow of celibacy. That was more than I could take. I borrowed the baptistery at an independent community church. I then joined that church, and so did they. There are things about my new church home that I do not like – such as instrumental music and women taking leading roles in the assembly. But on balance they seem to be much closer to the truth than the Church of Christ.

If God still hates divorce, as he did in Malachi 2:16, requiring that people get another divorce and break up another home would not seem to be what God would want. It is true that repentance must precede baptism, as taught in Acts 2:38. But repentance does not always mean restitution. Sometimes things cannot be restored to their original condition. There are times when there is no perfect solution. The best that can be done is to choose the option that does the least harm to all who are involved. Some church leaders have been in this situation in their personal evangelism efforts. They have told people that the best option for them would be to stop divorcing, make the most of their present marriage and teach their children not to get into this kind of situation.

I have, of course, heard this argument by analogy: "If a man steals his neighbor's mule and then repents, he cannot keep the mule. In the same way, if a man steals his neighbor's wife and then repents, he cannot keep her. He must give her back." That argument, however, always seemed to me to be flawed. A wife is not the same thing as a mule. A wife is a person, not a possession.

Both of the options presented to people in this kind of remarriage seem to me to be wrong. Going back to the first spouse would have been prohibited under the Law of Moses. Indeed, it was called "sin" and was said to be "an abomination before the LORD" (Deuteronomy 24:4). And some people do not have the gift of being able to live a celibate life according to what Paul wrote in 1 Corinthians 7:7-9. Congregations that take this position have never been very successful in persuading people to be baptized when the rule is that they must first divorce each other, remarry their first spouse or take a vow of celibacy.

## "A Divorced Fornicator Cannot Marry"

Here is the story told by one man:

> I destroyed my first marriage by my sexual immorality. I had sexual relations with several different women throughout those years. Eventually my wife divorced me, and I believe that she had the right to do that. Thank God we had no children to be hurt by my affairs. Several years after our divorce, my ex-wife married someone else. And I believe that she had the right to marry again. The man she married

> is a Christian. They now have three children. After being away from the Lord and from the church for more than 10 years, I saw what a mess I had made of my life. I was really sorry for my sins. I confessed my guilt to my ex-wife and to the church. At first the members of the church welcomed me back. But when I started dating, the minister told me that I could not marry again because in God's sight I was still married to my ex-wife. That did not seem right to me. I stopped going to church until I fell in love with a woman who is a member of another denomination. That church allowed me to marry again, and that is what I did. That is also why I am no longer a member of the Church of Christ.

A majority of people in Churches of Christ may believe that a divorced fornicator who repents can be forgiven but must never marry again. The only explanation of this doctrine that I have ever heard is that "in the sight of God the divorced fornicator is still married to that former spouse." I once heard some preachers discussing this issue, and one of them used an illustration that seemed to me to show the folly of this explanation. He took two dolls and tied them together with a string. Then he challenged the other preachers to cut that string in such a way that one doll would be free while the other doll would still be bound.

That illustration, of course, does not prove that a divorced fornicator who repents has the right to marry again. But it does show what is wrong with the reason given for this rule: that the divorced fornicator is still married to the first spouse in the sight of God although the innocent partner is free to marry again. I do not know of any reliable survey data on views in Churches of Christ concerning marriage and divorce issues, but it is my impression that a majority still teach that a divorced fornicator can never marry again. However, the small minority who no longer hold that view seems to be growing.

Some have come to believe that marriage is marriage – period. Those who are married according to the laws of the land where they live or according to the customs of their culture really are married and that includes being married "in the sight of God." Furthermore, they believe that divorce is divorce – period. Those who are divorced according to the laws of the land where they live or according to the customs of their culture really are divorced – not only according to human laws but they are no longer married to each other "in the sight of God."

Once I counseled with a couple who had divorced and were thinking about getting back together. I suggested that they start dating and go through the usual process of courtship while the counseling was going on. But on one of their dates, they had sexual intercourse. They justified their action with the claim that in the sight of God they were still married to each other. I told them that what they did was wrong – that it was fornication, extra-marital sexual intercourse, because they were no longer married to each other. I do not believe that people who have divorced according to the laws of the land where they live or the customs of their culture are still married to each other in the sight of God. Furthermore, I do not believe that people who are married to each other according to the laws or customs of their culture are really "living in adultery" in the sight of God. I do not find that language or that concept in Scripture.

## A Theology of Marriage

Before deciding which doctrine concerning divorce and remarriage to accept, one should first understand the theology of marriage. Consider once again how Jesus responded to the Pharisees who were trying to trap him by drawing him into their debate about the interpretation of what Moses wrote in Deuteronomy 24:1-4. Shammai taught that "he has found some indecency in her" (v. 1) referred to adultery and that was the only grounds for divorce. Hillel taught that if "then she finds no favor in his eyes because he has found some indecency in her" (v. 1) allowed divorce on any grounds.

In Mark's account (Mark 10:2-12), the question the Pharisees asked was, "Is it lawful for a man to divorce his wife?" (v. 2). Jesus responded by asking, "What did Moses command you?" (v. 3). Their answer was, "Moses allowed a man to write a certificate of divorce and to send her away" (v. 4) based on Deuteronomy 24:1-4. And Jesus briefly explained, "Because of your hardness of heart he wrote you this commandment" (Mark 10:5). What Jesus was talking about here, according to some scholars, is that it would be better to write a certificate of divorce and send her away so that she could marry someone else rather than to keep her in a marriage where spouse abuse and even murder would be likely. That is how hard their hearts had become. And that, some scholars believe, is why it would be wrong for her to return to that first husband. She would be getting back into a situation where abuse would likely continue. That, at least, is how some people in Churches of Christ see this.

But Jesus did not dwell on the explanation of what Moses wrote in Deuteronomy 24:1-4. Instead, he went back to what Moses wrote in the first few chapters of Genesis. He focused their attention on the creation purposes and covenant structure of marriage. That, I believe, is what we should do as we study the theology of marriage. There are, of course, several good studies concerning the theology of marriage. The problem has been with those who develop a doctrine of divorce and remarriage without considering and applying the insights from a theology of marriage.

A full discussion of the theology of marriage is beyond the scope of this book. Furthermore, others are far better qualified than I am to write about that theology. But if one goes back to the creation purposes of marriage in the first few chapters of Genesis, insights are obvious enough for any serious Bible student to recognize.

The first of these insights comes from Genesis 1:26 where God said, "Let us make man in our image, after our likeness. And let them have dominion over the fish of the sea and over the birds of the heavens and over the livestock and over all the earth and over every creeping thing that creeps on the earth." This is the first narrative in the Creation account that reflects a deliberative process of a relational God. There is something about humans that reflects the nature of God. But it is not the rugged individualism of one isolated person. It is, instead, the relationships that we have with one another. The God we serve is not one isolated being but rather a family-like relationship of three eternal persons: Father, Son and Holy Spirit – one God in three persons. In Genesis 2:18, God said, "It is not good that the man should be alone; I will make him a helper fit for him."

Back again to the Creation account in Genesis 1:27: "So God created man in his own image, in the image of God he created him; male and female he created them." Notice that both males and females are made in the image of God. Everything good about the nature of men and of women comes from God. Genesis 2:21-24 tells how that God made the first woman out of a rib taken from the side of Adam. When God brought the first woman to the first man he said, "This at last is bone of my bones and flesh of my flesh; she shall be called Woman, because she was taken out of Man" (v. 23). Then Moses wrote, "Therefore a man shall leave his father and his mother and hold fast to his wife, and they shall become one flesh" (v. 24). Before this creation narrative is finished, the first woman was called the "wife" of the first man (v. 25). This was the first marriage and the beginning of the first family.

As several writers have suggested, Eve was not made out of a bone taken from Adam's head, as though she should walk over him, nor of a bone taken from Adam's foot, as though he should walk over her. Instead, she was made of a bone taken from his side, from under his arm, suggesting that the two of them should walk through life as equals with Adam protecting and sheltering Eve.[2] That must surely have important implications for a theology of marriage.

Returning once more to the Creation account, we learn from Genesis 1:27 that God made humans "male and female." God's plan for marriage was one man and one woman going through life together. Regardless of what politicians and courts may say, a homosexual relationship of two men or two women is not marriage as God intended it to be. The first command that God gave to our first parents in Genesis 1:28 was, "Be fruitful and multiply and fill the earth and subdue it." That will not work in any homosexual relationship. It is only in the male-female relationship that children are conceived.

God created men and women with a powerful desire for sexual intimacy. That desire is normal and healthy. But God created marriage as a way of regulating the expression of that desire. It would be wrong to say that the only purpose of marriage is to produce children. But it is correct to say that God created marriage as the proper context for bringing children into the world and nurturing them. The duty of parents to care for their children must surely be seen as a part of the covenant obligations involved in marriage.

David P. Gushee, in his book *Getting Marriage Right* provided an outline of the creation purposes of marriage.[3] It was to provide:

Companionship:

- in work;
- in shared daily living; and
- in love

A context for giving sexual pleasure to each other;

A context for bringing children into the world and nurturing them; and

To function as the fundamental unit of society.

Gushee also bases his theology of marriage on the concept of covenant as the structural principle of marriage.[4] Marriage is more than a contract. It is a covenant relationship. Anything that breaks that covenant is a serious violation of God's purpose for marriage.

More and more writers who discuss divorce and remarriage are starting with the creation purposes and the covenant structure of marriage. Many of them regard extra-marital sexual intercourse as the most obvious form of covenant breaking but not necessarily the only grounds for divorce. Those who put the emphasis on covenant breaking say that no short, simple list of sins constitutes grounds for divorce. They say it is not that simple. Their approach is to consider things on a case-by-case basis. For them, the big question is, "Has the covenant relationship been damaged so much that it cannot be restored?"

When ministers and other counselors who take this approach deal with a couple considering divorce, they are very careful. First, they ask the couple to consider with an open mind the arguments presented by those who believe that the marriage relationship can be broken only by death. Then, if adultery has not been an issue with them, consider carefully the arguments presented by those who believe that adultery is the only grounds for divorce that would permit remarriage. If adultery is an issue, they urge the couple to consider seriously the possibility of forgiving the offense and working to rebuild the marriage relationship. Whatever has damaged the covenant relationship, they urge the couple to consider the possibility of rebuilding that relationship. They treat divorce as a last option. They do not teach that after a divorce one partner would be free to marry again while the other would still be married to the first spouse.

The exception language of Matthew 19:9 is a major challenge for those who believe that things other than adultery may break the covenant relationship and justify divorce. The more literal translations, such as the American Standard Version, reads, "Whoever shall put away his wife, except for fornication, and shall marry another, committeth adultery: and he that marrieth her when she is put away committeth adultery." That is the literal meaning of the Greek word "*pornia*." The New King James Version has "except for sexual immorality" with "fornication" as a marginal reference.

## Conclusion

These people who left Churches of Christ because of issues related to divorce and remarriage need to know that there are others in Churches of Christ who do not agree with positions taken by those who told them what they could or could not do.

It seems to me that Churches of Christ (and many other religious groups) have acted like debating societies assembled at the foot of a cliff waiting for people to fall on the rocks below. Then they debate the issue of whether to call for an ambulance or just shoot these people and put them out of their misery. The first thing I would want you to know is that I vote for the ambulance. But what is most important is that I vote for building a fence around the top of that cliff. Prevention rather than correction is the only way to solve the problem of ruined marriages and broken lives. We need to do far more than ever before to teach the next generation to build solid marriages. Churches also need to do much more to provide the teaching, instruction and counseling needed to strengthen marriages.

Chapter **8**

# Leadership Issues

"Laws are like sausages; it is better not to see them being made." That is what Otto von Bismarck, Iron Chancellor of Prussia, said about politics. At times it seems that the same thing could be said about church leadership. The average church member is not exposed to the less-flattering side of the leadership process. The closer a person gets to the inner workings of congregational life, the more that person is likely to conclude that the church must be a divine institution or it could never have survived its members and their leaders. Those who are most likely to accomplish good things in politics or in congregations are those who are willing to work with an imperfect system and with imperfect leaders. The ones most likely to do that are those who are humble enough to recognize their own imperfections.

Among those who responded to the "Why I Left Churches of Christ" survey were some who had been elders, deacons, preachers, youth ministers and teachers. Some left because of doctrinal differences. Most mentioned a variety of reasons. The things included in this chapter are some leadership issues given as one of the things that led to their decision to leave Churches of Christ.

## Views of Leadership

One former elder who left Churches of Christ mentioned some reasons for leaving that related to differences between what he understood church leadership to be and how other elders viewed church leadership. Here is a part of what he wrote:

> Soon after becoming an elder I discovered that there was a "head elder" in our church. He was the oldest of the elders and one of the original elders of that church. He probably worked harder than anyone else in the congregation. But he often made decisions without consulting the other elders. That was especially true in regard to money. The deacon who served as the treasurer was his son and he always did what his father told him to do. In my opinion, he had become a benevolent dictator. Some of his decisions seemed to me to be arbitrary and unjustified. I tried to change things, but the other elders refused to back me up. I asked this "head elder" to resign and explained why. He refused. He said that the Holy Spirit had made him an elder, and it would be wrong for him to resign. He believed that "once an elder always an elder."

Before discussing other things that this former elder said, I want to point out the "once an elder always an elder" view is not shared by elders in many Churches of Christ. Furthermore, the idea of one-man rule is clearly contradicted by the fact that all New Testament references to elders are in the plural. Churches should not tolerate an elder who acts like Diotrephes.[1] If the other elders will not correct him, the congregation should remove him.

The idea that the members of a congregation have the authority to remove an elder is not anything new. More than a century ago, David Lipscomb wrote a "Question and Answer" column in the *Gospel Advocate*. Someone wrote asking if the members of a congregation had the right to remove an elder who was no longer a faithful Christian. Lipscomb answered, "If the congregation had the right to appoint him in the first place it now surely has the right to disappoint him."

In Acts 20:28 Paul told the elders of the church in Ephesus, "Pay careful attention to yourselves and to all the flock, in which the Holy Spirit has made you overseers." Each elder is to keep watch over himself. Collectively the elders are to keep watch over the whole church. What some have missed is that elders need to keep watch over one another. Some elders have been reluctant to do this thinking that each elder answers only to God. But there is nothing in this passage that limits the application to individual responsibility or that would rule out any peer review of elders by other elders.

Some have used Acts 20:28 to support their claim that "once an elder always an elder." Because the Holy Spirit made them overseers, they claim that they cannot resign and that no one has the right to remove them from office. But the delegation, as I understand it, is not directly from the Holy Spirit to the elders. The delegation is first to the congregation as a whole and then to those the congregation selects to be the elders. A church that does not yet have elders has all the authority it needs to do everything a congregation is supposed to do. No new authority is created when a congregation first selects elders. What happens then is that some of the authority of the congregation as a whole is delegated to the elders. What is delegated can be withdrawn.

This former elder also objected to the way the elders went about selecting additional elders to join them in the eldership. The following is what he wrote:

> When one of the elders died and another moved away, the "head elder" decided that it was time to select some additional elders. I suggested that it should be the members of the congregation who did the selecting rather than the present elders. The other elders refused. They said, "If the members selected some men we did not want and we refused to appoint them – that would just cause hurt feelings and conflict."

The idea that the members should select their leaders is not a new idea. In 1870, J.W. McGarvey published *A Treatise on the Eldership*. He was editor of *Apostolic Times*, and this book is a collection of editorials that he wrote on the eldership. In this treatise, McGarvey argues that the selection model in Acts 6:1-7 should serve as a pattern for selecting all church leaders.

Throughout church history there have been three systems of church government. These can be distinguished by how each answers the question, "Who has the authority to select and to remove leaders in a local congregation?" The following are the three ways that question is answered:

1. In denominations with an Episcopalian structure, the bishop (or some official at the denominational headquarters) selects or removes leaders in a local congregation.
2. Denominations with a Presbyterian structure have such decisions made within the local church but not by the members. Those decisions are made by a self-perpetuating board of elders. When new elders are selected, the present elders select them.
3. A Congregational structure is one in which the members of the local church have the power to select and, if need be, remove leaders in their congregation.

Heirs of the Stone-Campbell Restoration Movement have historically rejected the practice of having any level of church organization above that of the local congregation. Churches of Christ and Christian Churches exist and function as informal fellowships of independent congregations. In the 1950s, the Christian Church (Disciples of Christ) was organized with a central denominational headquarters that speaks for all their congregations. However, that headquarters has little real control over local congregations. In all three of these Restoration Movement heirs, selection or removal of leaders is done within the local congregation. However, among congregations of all three Restoration Movement heirs, some have followed the Presbyterian model rather than the Congregational model when it comes to the selection of additional elders. The present elders are the ones who select additional elders in these congregations.

When this practice has been criticized, some elderships have allowed the members to nominate candidates for addition to the eldership. But the present elders decide which nominations to accept. In some cases it appears that they just accept the nominations of the ones they already wanted. The usual practice is to present the names of the candidates to the congregation and allow any member to present scriptural objections to any candidate that member does not believe to be qualified. Then the present elders decide which objections to sustain.

The practice of having the present elders select additional elders is one of the things that produce a kind of inbreeding. Elders have tended to select people similar to themselves. It is easier to get along with people whose personalities are similar to ours. But that practice goes against the biblical concept of the church as a body with many different members who have different gifts. A congregation needs that kind of diversity and so does an eldership.[2] The real problem here, of course, is a failure to understand the value of diversity. This kind of inbreeding could happen in a congregation where the members selected additional elders. It is just more likely to happen when the present elders select the additional elders.

A related issue is mentioned in the comments of another former elder. This is a part of what he wrote:

> A few years after I became an elder, two of the seven elders retired because of ill health; another died. We needed to select additional elders. It had been so long since two of the elders were appointed that there had been a major turnover in the membership. Most of the present members had not been in the congregation when those two were appointed. I talked to the other elders about the importance of an elder knowing that he served with the consent of the members. I suggested that when additional elders were selected it would be a good time for the present elders to be reaffirmed. The two older elders objected. One other elder and I wanted some kind of reaffirmation. But the best compromise that we could get was that when the congregation was asked if they had any scriptural objection to the appointment of the new elders, they would also be told that if they had any scriptural reason why any of the present elders should not continue in office, they could submit their objection in a signed letter. Then the elders would decide whether to sustain that objection. I said that any member of the church always has a right to raise a scriptural objection to any elder continuing to serve.

> Simply because we reminded the members of this right did not give the elders any way of knowing that the members still wanted them to continue serving as elders.

There were other reasons for this former elder's decision to leave Churches of Christ. This was just one example of what he saw as an authoritarian leadership style. Fortunately most elderships in Churches of Christ are not like that. I really think that the trend is away from an authoritarian style and toward a more open and transparent kind of leadership.

In the mid-1980s when I wrote *Church Leadership and Organization*, I was concerned about dangers from two opposite extremes. Chapter 2 was on "The Error of an Authoritarian Leadership Style."[3] The subject in Chapter 3 was "The Error of Changing the Structure of Church Organization."[4] One of the dangers that I was talking about in Chapter 3 came from a doctrine being advanced at several Soul Winning Workshops. According to this doctrine, "Elders do not have the right to fire a preacher without the majority consent of the members." Furthermore, some of the advocates of this position denied that the elders have any decision-making role at all. According to this view, elders are just supposed to lead by persuasion and example, but decisions are to be made by the majority vote of the members. Later, however, I saw two even more extreme dangers. One was from the Discipling Movement that, in my opinion, had gone beyond authoritarianism and developed a system of totalitarian control.[5] An opposite extreme had developed among a few who affirmed that there was no need for elders, church treasuries or congregational assemblies. People are supposed to be good Christians on their own. If they ever feel the need for fellowship with other Christians, they could just invite a few others to come to their house. I discussed all of these extremes in a chapter that I wrote on "Recent Trends in Church Leadership." That chapter was included in *Directions for the Road Ahead: Stability and Change among Churches of Christ*.[6] I believe the trend away from an authoritarian leadership has continued to the present time. There is a growing awareness of the need for elders to be shepherds and not just decision-makers. There is also more emphasis on the need for elders to delegate decision-making authority to deacons, ministers and others working under the supervision of the overseers.

## Three Leadership Roles

In the responses to the "Why I Left Churches of Christ" survey, six had previously served as full-time church-supported ministers: four preachers and two youth ministers. A common theme in their responses was a complaint about elders functioning only as a decision-making body but expecting the church-supported ministers to fill the pastoral role. Typical of these essay responses was a preacher quoted below:

> When I first started preaching, I corrected people who called me "pastor." After a few years I gave up that effort because I was doing far more pastoral work than the elders were. I was expected to visit the sick, visit all of the members, do pre-marriage and marriage counseling, and other kinds of counseling that fulfill the spiritual counseling/teaching role implied by the term shepherd or pastor.

In recent years a growing number of elders have come to recognize the three leadership roles they are supposed to perform. However, in many Churches of Christ, the way people pray for their leaders reveals an inadequate understanding of the three leadership roles. Most of the time when the prayer is for God to bless these leaders they call them "elders," not "overseers" or "shepherds." And almost always that is followed with the plea for God to help them make good decisions. Decision-making is about all that many members of the church associate with the role of elders.

Unfortunately, some congregations of the Churches of Christ in the United States accepted the view of church leadership as limited to the decision-making done by elders at the top of an organizational chart. They are the ones who make all the decisions. Deacons are at the next level, but they just do what they are told to do and have little if any decision-making authority. Church-supported ministers are in staff positions rather than line positions. They also have little if any involvement in the decision-making process, but they are usually expected to perform the pastoral duties.

## The Importance of Delegation

A former deacon who left Churches of Christ gave as one of his reasons for leaving: After he was asked to serve as a deacon, he was never given anything meaningful to do. Here is a part of what he wrote:

> I used to be a very active member of the church. Then they appointed me as a deacon. I thought that the elders would plan the overall program of church work and delegate to deacons the day-to-day operational management of the various ministries. I was assigned to be one of several deacons working in the Education Ministry. However, there was one elder in charge of that ministry. When members of the congregation had comments, criticism, complaints or suggestions about the Bible classes, they always went to that elder. I doubt that they even knew which deacons worked with the various ministries.

That former deacon said that he taught management courses in the School of Business Administration at a nearby state university. Here is a part of what he wrote about the difference between what is taught and what he saw practiced in the church where he was a deacon:

> The elders told the three of us who served as deacons working in the Education Ministry that they were delegating to us the responsibility for the Bible classes. However, they never delegated any decision-making authority to us. In my classes at the university, I tell my students that administrators cannot delegate responsibility. All they can delegate is decision-making authority. When they delegate decision-making authority they are still personally responsible for everything their divisions are supposed to do, but now they are also responsible for training and supervising those working under their oversight.

He went on to say that working as a deacon gave him a closer view than he had ever had before of how the eldership functioned. Here is a part of what he wrote:

> Before I was appointed as a deacon, I had always assumed that the elders focused their decision-making on

> matters of strategic importance and that they delegated to deacons the tactical matters of day-to-day operational management. But from what I observed after I became a deacon, it seemed to me that the elders spent most of their time doing things that could and should have been delegated to deacons.

What that former deacon complained about is exactly what I have observed in most of the congregations where I have worked as a church consultant. I am now on my third "tour of duty" as a deacon. All three times it has been in great congregations where the elders really try to focus on strategic issues. But in these congregations the elders would admit that they spend far too much time "putting out fires" and not enough time clarifying the congregation's vision. I must confess, however, that earlier when I served as an elder we did the same thing. Often it seemed easier in the short run to do things ourselves rather than to delegate, train, supervise and motivate deacons who could then tend to those things. We knew that in the long run it would be far better to empower deacons, ministers and others to do the day-to-day operational management. We knew that we should focus our efforts on planning far beyond next year's budget. We just did not have the time or the energy to do it that way. And after all, when you have a fire, putting it out is a good thing to do.

I am not among those who have left Churches of Christ because of these leadership matters, but I can understand the frustration. My personal observation is that in far too many Churches of Christ, the elders are doing deacons' work; the deacons have very little to do; and the church-supported ministers do most of the pastoral work. If strategic planning is done at all, it is done by ministers. However, some of these former church leaders who responded to this survey admitted that after they left Churches of Christ and joined another religious group, they encountered the very same problems.

## Questions About Power

When Reuel Lemmons edited the *Firm Foundation*, he wrote several editorials on the question "Who Calls the Shots?" There was an exchange of articles arguing about the "power" of elders and ministers. One of the things that I found to be useful in studying this subject was the analysis of "Social Power" by four social psychologists.[7] Position Power includes power by virtue of office, reward power, coercion power and control of information. Personal Power includes persuasion, the influence of personal example, charisma and the trust based on expertise.

Do elders have legitimate power – power by virtue of office? I believe they do because some of the power of the congregation as a whole was delegated to them when the members selected them as elders. But when I have conducted leadership seminars I have told elders that their power to lead comes from a reservoir of goodwill, and they can drain that tank in a hurry. Do elders have the right to fire a preacher without the majority consent of the members? I believe that they do. I know of cases in which that is what the elders had to do. In one case a preacher was found to be guilty of homosexual immorality. He repented and was forgiven, but the elders believed that he could not remain as their preacher. They knew that he needed to get into a completely different environment. But they wanted to protect that preacher's future usefulness in ministry. They got some good counseling for the preacher. That counseling helped put his marriage back together. He left that congregation and had several years of fruitful labor as a preacher elsewhere. But it would have destroyed his future usefulness in ministry if they had told the congregation why they fired that preacher. So they told the members, "You will just have to trust us on this matter." When I have discussed this subject in leadership classes, I have said that elders can get away with that about one time in a row. That is not how things should usually be done.

Did Paul have legitimate power by virtue of his position as an apostle so that he could command Philemon to welcome his runaway slave, Onesimus, back "no longer as a slave but more than a slave, as a beloved brother" (Philemon 1:16)? I believe that he did. He said that he had that kind of authority. But is that the way Paul tried to persuade Philemon? Absolutely not! Paul's short letter to Philemon is a model of strong but gentle persuasion. That is the way elders ought to lead the church.

I believe that the following paragraph from my chapter on "Trends in Church Leadership" is worth repeating here: Tom Yokum did a word study that included the Greek words for (1) the positions of a leader;

(2) the functions of a leader; and (3) the responses to leaders. His study notes which words were used, were not used or were rejected in the New Testament. He concludes that the words for power by virtue of position are specifically rejected for church leaders and the only words that are used with approval are those for personal power.[8]

Position Power is not how elders should lead a church. It is not right for elders to lord it over the church, but it is just as bad for preachers to lord it over the church. Preachers have the power of the Word. To use the title of a book by Fred Craddock, preachers should lead *As One Without Authority*.[9]

The New Testament pattern, as I understand it, is that the most important decisions that have an impact on the whole church were to be made by those in closest touch with the needs of the members because of their work as shepherds. Also those strategic decisions were to be made by those most in touch with the full range of congregational activities because of their work as overseers. It is a mistake to split off the decision-making function of elders from the administrative function of overseers and the spiritual counseling/teaching function of shepherds.

Church leadership is not about the power of the leaders. Instead, it is about empowering the members. According to Ephesians 4:11, Christ "gave the apostles, the prophets, the evangelists, the shepherds and teachers" with the primary function "to equip the saints for the work of ministry, for building up the body of Christ" (v. 12). It was the apostles and prophets who established the early churches and wrote the books of the New Testament as our guide. The "saints" in the New Testament included all of the Christians. There was no clergy-laity distinction. All Christians were called to be ministers. They were all called to be "priests" (1 Peter 2:4-11; Revelation 1:6). That included both men and women, young and old. The primary function of the leaders was to help the members discover their gifts and get involved in some areas of ministry in the priesthood of the believers. Would that it were so today.

Here is what one of the former preachers who responded to this survey said about the elders in the congregations where he had served:

> In both of the congregations where I preached before leaving the Churches of Christ, I never saw any initiative that came

> from the elders. They just functioned as a "Veto Board" telling the rest of us what we could not do. All of the proposals for improving the work of the church came from me, from some of the deacons, or from some other members. It was as though they were trying to drive a bus without being able to steer or step on the gas. All that they could do was to step on the brakes.

Church leadership is not about control. Control is a sick way of relating to people.

## Why Ministers Are Leaving

Only six responses to this survey came from people who had been full-time, church-supported ministers (four preachers and two youth ministers). That is a very small sample. However, some of their reasons for leaving Churches of Christ were very similar to responses in two very large samples. The first of these studies was conducted around 30 years ago. Waymon Miller was preparing for a program at Harding University in what was called the "Thirteen-in-One Seminar." His assigned topic was "Why Ministers Are Leaving." He had prepared a list of more than 1,000 mature men who had served successfully for several years as full-time church-supported ministers. All of these men were still members of the Churches of Christ, but they had left that kind of ministry. Waymon was in that situation himself. After years of faithful service as a missionary in South Africa, he then preached for several congregations in the United States. The last of these was the Park Plaza Church of Christ in Tulsa, Okla. After leaving that pulpit ministry, Waymon owned a printing company. Back then I was the chairman of the speech communication program at the University of Tulsa. Waymon knew that I had been trained in survey research. He asked me to help construct a survey form and do the statistical analysis. Results of that study showed that the two main reasons ministers were leaving full-time church-supported ministry were: (1) problems in dealing with elders or other church leaders; and (2) inadequate financial support – especially the lack of any retirement plans or insurance.

In the fall of 2000, I conducted a survey. This was not of ministers who had left Churches of Christ or even of ministers who had left full-time church-supported ministry. But it was of people who had seriously thought about leaving that kind of ministry. The two main reasons that I found in that study were the very same as what Waymon Miller found 20 years earlier. Here are some of the comments from the present study and those two earlier studies:

> The elders regarded me as their "employee" rather than as a "partner in ministry." After spending years of preparation for ministry that included an undergraduate degree in Bible, and three years of graduate study leading to the master's of divinity degree – I found that my work in ministry was being controlled by men who had far less knowledge of the Bible or of ministry.
>
> In both of the Churches of Christ where I preached after graduating from school, the elders over-reacted to criticism. When people went to the elders with criticism about me, they never defended me as though I was their partner in ministry. I was just the "hired help." The people who complained were the "customers." And it was my job to keep the customers happy. Those elders regarded the absence of complaints as evidence of good leadership. But a graveyard is a place where no one complains, and that is not what things are like in a healthy church.
>
> I knew that there must be a pastoral dimension to the work of a preacher. I understood that the elders were not supported as I was so that I could devote my full time to my ministry. What bothered me was how seldom there was a pastoral dimension to the work of the elders. It seems that we have rewritten James 5:14 so that now it says, "Is any one of you sick? Let the preacher visit him. That is a part of what he is being paid to do."
>
> I had only one regularly scheduled meeting with the elders each year. That was when they told me whether they wanted me to remain as their preacher for another year. The only other times when I met with the elders were when they

> wanted to complain about something I had done or said. They believed that it was their duty to conduct my "performance review." That was when they told me all the ways in which I needed to improve. And their comments were not limited to my work as a minister. They told me about all the ways in which my wife and our children needed to improve. After I finally got fed up with their way of relating to me, I asked them when they wanted me in my role as an evangelist to tell them all the ways in which they and their families needed to improve. They never got around to scheduling that meeting, but at least it ended my performance reviews for the remainder of my tenure with that congregation – which, incidentally, was not very long.

I never had nerve enough to try that approach, although I now believe that there were times when I probably should have. I suppose that I was afraid that doing so would be like preaching a very moving sermon – the kind that you preach and then move. I "tried out" one time for a preaching position with a congregation located very close to a large state university known for its football teams. The elders of that church used football language to describe the role of their pulpit minister. They called him "the quarterback of our team." I asked how often they met with their preacher. They said, "Once a year to let him know whether we were renewing his contract for another year." I told those elders that I grew up in Dallas, Texas, where Tom Landry coached the Dallas Cowboys football team. Even though they had some really great quarterbacks, Landry always had the plays called from the bench. I said, "I have no problem with the elders calling the plays, but if I am going to be the quarterback I at least want to be in the huddle. I don't need to have a vote, but I at least need to have a voice." They decided to get a different quarterback.

## Conclusion

The people discussed in this chapter left Churches of Christ, at least in part, because of their dissatisfaction on leadership issues. Reading their expressions of dissatisfaction, of course, is like hearing only one side of the story. If we could talk to the elders in those congregations, they might tell a very different story. But in this survey because we asked these people to explain why they left, we should assume some validity is in their complaints. Not many people brought up these leadership issues, but this may just be the tip of the iceberg. I have seen congregations where only a few people were complaining, but a much larger group had already voted with their feet and their vote was one of "no confidence" in the present leadership. Exit interviews are used in many organizations. And when people tell us why they left, we really ought to listen. If we do, we just might learn something.

Chapter **9**

# Evangelism Issues

None of the people who responded to this survey said that their primary reason for leaving was what Churches of Christ taught about evangelism. However, several of the responses at least mentioned this subject. Some complained about how the preachers in the Churches of Christ they had attended used guilt and fear appeals in their efforts to persuade more members of the church to be more active in personal evangelism. The following are some things they said – along with my reflections.

## Comments About Evangelism

> Before I decided to leave Churches of Christ, our preacher took some of us to a Soul Winning Workshop. One of the main speakers said, "The gospel of Christ is absolutely irresistible. There is no way that anyone can turn it down if you just present it right. So if people you are trying to convert do not obey, it is your fault. You must have said something wrong or left something out." I did not agree with that speaker, but our preacher did. Something that he often said was, "You can't go to heaven alone. If you don't take

> someone with you, you can't get in." When I left Churches of Christ, I joined a church that is just as evangelistic but without making false claims like that.

Those claims do not reflect what most people in Churches of Christ believe. They certainly do not reflect what I have taught in my evangelism classes at Harding and in workshops conducted for congregations throughout the United States and Canada. What I have taught and what I am persuaded most Churches of Christ teach is that there are three parts to conversion: (1) what God does; (2) what the evangelist does; and (3) what the convert does. If you leave out God's part, evangelism becomes nothing more than a human effort to persuade – mere salesmanship. If you leave out the convert's part, evangelism becomes manipulation in which the prospective convert is like a puppet with the evangelist pulling the strings. Of course, if you leave out the evangelist's part, the Great Commission becomes the Great Omission. People have free will. They have the power of choice. And they are personally responsible for those choices.

Many books on evangelism use high pressure salesmanship as the model. They even use the jargon: "finding prospects," "getting your foot in the door," "establishing a need," "dealing with objections" and "closing the sale." But most members of the Churches of Christ have rejected this approach to evangelism. Some grew up thinking that evangelism had to be manipulation; they just decided to serve in other ways and not to be involved in evangelism. That is why I have tried to get people thinking about evangelism in a different way.

## Unconscious Assumptions Reflected in the Way We Speak

The way people talk often betrays their unconscious assumptions. When people talk about conversion, they use the active voice to describe the role of the evangelist. That is accurate because evangelism is something that we do. But when people talk about the role of the convert, many of them switch to the passive voice. They do not ask, "When did you convert?" Instead they ask, "When were you converted?" or "Who converted you?" That is wrong because converting is something that people do, not something that an evangelist does to them. Christian evangelism is not a manipulative monologue like high pressure salesmanship. It is a non-manipulative dialogue – a friendly conversation.

The King James Version often uses the passive voice to describe the role of the convert. Some people take that as justification for their use of the passive voice when talking about what is the role of the convert. But the original Greek text of the New Testament always uses the active voice to describe the role of the convert – not the passive voice. In 1611 when the King James Version was translated as the "Authorized Version" for use in the Church of England, that church had been highly influenced by Calvinism. Martin Bucer of Strassbourg was a disciple of Huldrych Zwingli, the founder of the Reformed Church tradition. He was a contemporary of John Calvin. Bucer was a professor of divinity at Cambridge University. In 1550 he presented his book, *The Reign of Christ*, to King Edward VI. Bucer was the primary influence in bringing Calvinism to England.

The scholars who produced the King James Version were required to translate the original Greek text in a way that was consistent with doctrines and practices in the Church of England. That is why they used the transliterated word "baptize" instead of the literal translation, "immerse." That is also why they used the passive voice for the role of the convert. Calvin taught that converting is not something that the convert does. It is something that God does to the convert by a direct operation of the Holy Spirit separate and apart from the influence of God's Word revealed in the Bible. Calvin was right in not ignoring God's role in conversion, but he was wrong in ignoring the role and the responsibility of the convert. People today who use the active voice to describe the role of the evangelist and the passive voice to describe the role of the convert are right in recognizing the role of the evangelist, but they are wrong in ignoring the role and the responsibility of the convert. This subtle point about grammar may reflect an unconscious assumption about the nature of evangelism.

## A Parable Misused

Here is another comment that shows the need for correcting unconscious assumptions.

> The preacher in the congregation where I grew up often said, "The only fruit of a Christian is another Christian. If

> you are not bearing fruit by making converts, God will cut you down and cast you into the fire." I told him that he was misusing the Parable of the Vine and the Branches. What I said was, "In John 15, Christ is the vine and Christians are the branches. But if the only fruit of a Christian is another Christian, then the only fruit of a branch is another branch. Where are the grapes?" He had no answer.

One way I tried to correct this false assumption was in an article that I wrote for the *Christian Worker*. The title was "A Parable of the Trees." It went something like this:

> Once upon a time there was a land where all sorts of trees grew. They produced an abundant harvest of fruit. There was plenty of food for everyone, and everyone was happy. But then a false prophet came into that land. He conducted a Tree-Growing Workshop. He preached to the trees and he said, "The only fruit of a tree is another tree. And you lazy good-for-nothing trees have not been meeting your quota for producing new trees. If you don't repent, God will cast you into the fire and burn you up." One wise old tree said, "Wait a minute, young man. The fruit of the apple tree is its apples. The fruit of the pear tree is its pears. The fruit of the cherry tree is its cherries. The fruit contains the seed, and the seed falls into the ground. But whether new trees grow depends on the soil where the seed comes to rest. We cannot control that." But the false prophet refused to listen to the wise old tree. He banged on his Bible and yelled repeatedly, "The only fruit of a tree is another tree." When they sang the invitation song – all verses of Just As I Am repeated several times – all of the trees came forward and confessed their negligence in focusing on things like apples, pears and cherries. They promised to go home and work as hard as they could to sprout new trees out of their branches. What happened the following year was that the production of new trees fell off sharply. But there was a major increase in the incidence of hypertension (high sap pressure?); 30 percent of the trees grew ulcers, and 20 percent of them had nervous breakdowns.

My hope was that the readers would get the point. It is not correct to say that the only fruit of a Christian is another Christian. We are supposed to bear the fruit of a Christlike example, and we are also supposed to bear the fruit of proclamation. If we tell others about Jesus and they refuse to believe and obey, we should grieve for them – but we should not borrow their guilt. Most of the Churches of Christ that I know do not try to manipulate the members in an effort to persuade them to be more active in personal evangelism.

Here is more of what the former member quoted earlier had to say:

> I went to [my preacher] one time with a long list of other ways in which the Bible uses the "fruit" metaphor. He said that all of those other things were the fruit of the Spirit, and converts are the only fruit that Christians bear. I thought that his explanation ignored the role of the Spirit in conversion and implied that the fruit of the Spirit is produced in us without any effort on our part.

There are places in the New Testament where the related words for "harvest" and "fruit" are used metaphorically for the converts who come as a result of evangelism. "The harvest is plentiful, but the laborers are few; therefore pray earnestly to the Lord of the harvest to send out laborers into his harvest" (Matthew 9:37-38). "Do you not say, 'There are yet four months, then comes the harvest'? Look, I tell you, lift up your eyes, and see that the fields are white for harvest. Already the one who reaps is receiving wages and gathering fruit for eternal life" (John 4:35-36). Paul could have used the word "fruit" with reference to converts in such passages as Romans 1:13 and Philippians 1:22. But it is quite clear that New Testament writers often used the word "fruit" where the reference was not about making converts. Note the kinds of "fruit" mentioned in the following passages:

- "sanctification" (Romans 6:22)
- "love, joy, peace, patience, kindness, goodness, faithfulness, gentleness, self-control" (Galatians 5:22-23)
- "all that is good and right and true" (Ephesians 5:9)
- "righteousness" (Philippians 1:11; James 3:18)
- "the peaceful fruit of righteousness"(Hebrews 12:11)

- contributions sent to a missionary (Philippians 4:17)
- "every good work" (Colossians 1:10)
- "praise" (Hebrews 13:15)

If someone tells you that "the only fruit of a Christian is another Christian," show them all these other ways in which the New Testament uses that metaphor.

## Comments About a Better Way

> I do not have the gift of evangelism. I try to set the right example, and I tell others about Jesus – but I am not really a soul winner. In the Church of Christ that I attended, the preacher tried to get all of us to attend his Personal Evangelism Training Class. He insisted that we spend every Saturday knocking doors to set up Bible studies. I tried a few times, but I really was not cut out for that kind of work. That is not why I left the Church of Christ, but after I joined another church I noticed a clear contrast between the two in relation to evangelism. The church that I joined practices what they call "team evangelism." They say that the Great Commission was not limited to the apostles, but it applies to the church as a whole body and not to any one individual. They say that we cannot all be "soul winners," but we can all be "witnesses." They use a "stair-step" approach to evangelism. Some Christians use whatever gifts they have to serve others in the name of Christ. Through this service they build relationships in which they witness by telling others about Jesus. That helps people go up the first step. Several other Christians might be needed to bring them up the next few steps. Finally a "soul winner" persuades them to pray the Sinner's Prayer and accept Jesus into their hearts.

That "team evangelism" and "stair-step" approach are exactly what I have taught for years in my seminars on evangelistic church growth. Churches of Christ do not use the same language about "witnessing," but this is basically what most Churches of Christ teach and practice. There is, of course, an obvious difference when it comes to what people must do to be saved. We do not tell people to pray the "Sinner's Prayer" because that prayer has no biblical foundation. We want people to invite Jesus into their hearts and to accept Jesus as their personal Savior. That is a part of what faith involves. But when people get to this point, we tell them to repent and be baptized for the forgiveness of their sins – because that is what the apostles taught (Acts 2:38).

Several years ago a researcher at Mormon headquarters in Salt Lake City called me with a question about some statistics that I reported in a journal article. After I answered his question, I had a question for him. I told him that in 1950 when I started preaching, Churches of Christ had twice as many members in the United States as the Mormons. Today the Mormons have twice as many members as we have. I was curious about the source of their growth. I told him that I had seen their 18-year-old "elders" going door to door. But I told him that Churches of Christ have not found door-to-door canvassing to be very successful. We still do it because in some cases it is the only way to get a new mission work started, but we make very few converts by that method. I asked him what they did that made door-to-door canvassing productive. He said, "It is not very productive for us either. We may make one convert for every 3,000 doors those young people knock on." He went on to say they continue using door-to-door canvassing because it is good training for their young "elders," and they occasionally make a convert through that method of contact. So I asked him, "Where is your growth coming from?" He replied, "We are having many more babies than you people are having, but the main thing is that we have found that we make one convert for every two people we have into our homes for a meal." It seems to me that this is a good example of how important the interpersonal context is in evangelism.

One of my father's first cousins grew up as a Methodist. He went to medical school and became a radiologist. He moved to the Seattle area where he joined a team of radiologists who were all Mormons. This cousin had a fire that destroyed his home. The local Mormon church took care of his family after the fire. That service (*diakonia*) brought him and his family even more into the friendship circle (*koinonia*) of these Mormons. Today he is a Sunday-School teacher for the Mormons. I do not think they converted him by telling him their doctrines. I think that he absorbed their belief system in the context of his relationships.

Here is another comment from this survey:

> When I was a member of the Church of Christ, I found that most of the so-called evangelism was really just proselytizing. Almost all of the effort was spent debating other Christians. The church that I joined when I left the Church of Christ tries to reach the unchurched. In most of our evangelism we target the unbelievers.

This is another area that is exactly what I have taught for many years. I am not ready to give up on a dialogue with other believers. If they are right, we are wrong on the issues where we differ; and if we are right, they are wrong. That dialogue needs to continue. But many years of doing statistical research on patterns of growth and decline among Churches of Christ in the United States has convinced me that few converts are coming from our dialogue with other believers. They have not proven to be a very receptive audience. Most of the converts had no previous religious affiliation.

## A Change of Methods

When I was growing up, many church members thought that fulfilling the Great Commission involved little more than having two gospel meetings each year, a debate every other year and frequent door-knocking campaigns. The regular church schedule involved preaching services every Sunday morning, Sunday evening, and often on Wednesday evening. Most of the sermons were on doctrinal differences between Churches of Christ and other believers. There was much numerical growth among Churches of Christ back then, but that growth may have been in spite of that strategy.

Not too many years ago, most of the people around us already believed in God, in Jesus Christ as the Son of God and in the Bible as the inspired Word of God. People already knew that those who are lost in sin need to be saved. The debate was about what people needed to do to be saved. We could begin at that point and use proof-text reasoning to persuade people to be baptized. Today, most of the people around us are not sure what they believe. Many have unconsciously accepted the world view of postmodernism and assume that there is no absolute truth in matters of beliefs, values and morals. Most are functionally unbelievers who are biblically illiterate. It takes a different evangelism strategy to reach people in this culture today. The gospel has not changed, and the spiritual needs of people have not changed. But the culture around us has changed, and the starting point for evangelism must also change.

The fundamental doctrines of Churches of Christ have not changed. Strategies, however, have changed. Approaches and methods used by most Churches of Christ today are not the same as what they were in previous generations. Pioneers of the Stone-Campbell Restoration Movement often used a slogan that came from Thomas Campbell's "Declaration and Address": "In matters of faith – unity; in matters of opinion – liberty; and in all things – charity." Because "faith comes by hearing, and hearing by the word of God" (Romans 10:17 NKJV), a matter of faith, by definition, is a matter that the Bible clearly teaches and upon which we should all be able to agree. A matter of opinion, by contrast, is a matter that the Bible does not clearly teach one way or the other, and Christians may differ in their understanding. Problems come, however, when one person's matter of faith is another person's matter of opinion. In these matters of personal conviction and conscience, charity is most needed. We must be humble enough to differ without dividing, disagree without being disagreeable, and discuss without discord.

## Disciple-Making and Disciple-Building

Evangelism is usually thought of as persuading people to become Christians. But in the Great Commission Jesus not only said, "[M]ake disciples of all nations," He also said, "teaching them to observe all that I have commanded you" (Matthew 28:19-20). The Greek text, however, simply uses a verb form of the noun "disciple." Literally the command is to "disciple all people." The reference is not to nations as political institutions. It is to all different kinds of people groups. The single verb "disciple" includes two different parts of one process: disciple-making and disciple-building. The second includes efforts to teach Christians and to restore those who fall away.

> Brothers, if anyone is caught in any transgression, you who are spiritual should restore him in a spirit of gentleness. Keep

> watch on yourself, lest you too be tempted. Bear one another's burdens, and so fulfill the law of Christ (Galatians 6:1-2).

> My brothers, if anyone among you wanders from the truth and someone brings him back, let him know that whoever brings back a sinner from his wandering will save his soul from death and will cover a multitude of sins (James 5:19-20).

In this effort, it is important to recognize that some cannot be brought back to repentance.

## Why Some Cannot Be Brought Back to Repentance

Calvinists affirm a doctrine of "once saved always saved." They have a hard time explaining Hebrews 6:4-6, although the language is very clear:

> For it is impossible, in the case of those who have once been enlightened, who have tasted the heavenly gift, and have shared in the Holy Spirit, and have tasted the goodness of the word of God and the powers of the age to come, and then have fallen away, to restore them again to repentance, since they are crucifying once again the Son of God to their own harm and holding him up to contempt.

Second Peter 2:20-22 is another passage that is hard for Calvinists to explain:

> For if, after they have escaped the defilements of the world through the knowledge of our Lord and Savior Jesus Christ, they are again entangled in them and overcome, the last state has become worse for them than the first. For it would have been better for them never to have known the way of righteousness than after knowing it to turn back from the holy commandment delivered to them. What the true proverb says has happened to them: "The dog returns to its own vomit, and the sow, after washing herself, returns to wallow in the mire."

Another passage affirms the same thing: "You are severed from Christ, you who would be justified by the law; you have fallen away from grace" (Galatians 5:4).

When people harden their hearts to the influence of God's Word, some cross a point of no return. The story of God's love manifested in the sacrifice of Jesus Christ rolls off them like water off a duck's back. In that condition people cannot be reached. Christians should grieve for them but not borrow their guilt. If you are like me, you have real personal guilt. You most certainly do not need to borrow the guilt that properly belongs to someone else.

What these Scriptures teach is true, but we do not know when someone has passed that point of no return. Therefore, we do not give up hope as long as there is life. In keeping with 1 John 5:16-17, we do not pray for God to pardon the sins of those who died while alienated from him. But we keep on praying and seeking to persuade those who are still living.

The New Testament clearly teaches that some who have fallen away cannot be brought to repentance. But it also teaches that some people who have not yet become Christians cannot be brought to faith in Christ. This is a hard thing for some Christians to accept, but the New Testament clearly teaches a doctrine of election – not Calvin's doctrine of "particular election," but rather a doctrine of "general election."

## General Election

Some heirs of the Stone-Campbell Restoration Movement may have gone so far in their rejection of Calvin's doctrine of "particular election" that they have ignored the biblical doctrine of "general election." Understanding this important Bible doctrine about some who have never become members of the church may also help Christians to have the correct understanding regarding some of those who have left.

The doctrine of "general election" affirms a category of people who are predestined to be saved. Those who honestly seek to know the truth will believe it when they hear it. They have been chosen by God. They are the "elect" (Mark 13:20). But in this election, "God votes for you, the devil votes against you, and which way you vote determines where you will go."

In Calvinism, conversion is totally explained by the role of a sovereign God. Calvinism has no emphasis or clear understanding concerning the role of the Christian evangelist or the role of the convert. In Churches of Christ, however, some have left out both God's part and the convert's part. That may explain why some members of the Churches of Christ have ignored the biblical doctrine of "general election." But the New Testament is filled with passages that clearly teach this doctrine.

> I know that you are offspring of Abraham; yet you seek to kill me because my word finds no place in you (John 8:37).
>
> Why do you not understand what I say? It is because you cannot bear to hear my word (John 8:43).
>
> Whoever is of God hears the words of God. The reason why you do not hear them is that you are not of God (John 8:47).
>
> [Y]ou do not believe because you are not part of my flock (John 10:26).

When Luke reports the preaching by Paul and Barnabas in Pisidian Antioch, he concludes by writing, "[A]s many as were appointed to eternal life believed" (Acts 13:48). Notice the order: being appointed for eternal life came before believing.

In the early days of Paul's ministry in Corinth, the Lord appeared to him in a vision and said, "Do not be afraid, but go on speaking and do not be silent, for I am with you, and no one will attack you to harm you, for I have many in this city who are my people" (Acts 18:9-10).

Those who do not understand the doctrine of general election might argue with the Lord, "How can you use the present tense and say that you have many people in this city? These people have not even heard the gospel message. They have not yet believed and repented. They have not yet been baptized." But the Lord might reply, "I know the hearts of people. Even in this wicked city, there are many honest seekers. I already know that when they hear the gospel, they will believe, obey and be saved. That is why I can already claim them as "my people."

In Romans 8:28-30 Paul wrote:

> And we know that for those who love God all things work together for good, for those who are called according to his

> purpose. For those whom he foreknew he also predestined to be conformed to the image of his Son, in order that he might be the firstborn among many brothers. And those whom he predestined he also called, and those whom he called he also justified, and those whom he justified he also glorified.

In 1 Corinthians 1:18, Paul explained why some people are receptive to the gospel while others are not. "For the word of the cross is folly to those who are perishing, but to us who are being saved it is the power of God."

Paul also explained, "The natural person does not accept the things of the Spirit of God, for they are folly to him, and he is not able to understand them because they are spiritually discerned" (1 Corinthians 2:14). Then in 2 Corinthians 2:14-17, Paul wrote:

> But thanks be to God, who in Christ always leads us in triumphal procession, and through us spreads the fragrance of the knowledge of him everywhere. For we are the aroma of Christ to God among those who are being saved and among those who are perishing, to one a fragrance from death to death, to the other a fragrance from life to life. Who is sufficient for these things? For we are not, like so many, peddlers of God's word, but as men of sincerity, as commissioned by God, in the sight of God we speak in Christ.

In 2 Corinthians 4:3-4, Paul wrote:

> And even if our gospel is veiled, it is veiled only to those who are perishing. In their case the god of this world has blinded the minds of the unbelievers, to keep them from seeing the light of the gospel of the glory of Christ, who is the image of God.

In 2 Thessalonians 2:10-12, Paul explained why some are perishing:

> [A]nd with all wicked deception for those who are perishing, because they refused to love the truth and so be saved. Therefore God sends them a strong delusion, so that they may believe what is false, in order that all may be condemned who did not believe the truth but had pleasure in unrighteousness.

These passages shed light on the nature of evangelism. It is not our responsibility to convert the whole world. The task that God sets before us is to present the gospel message as clearly and as persuasively as possible to as many people as we can. We do this with the understanding that only the honest truth seekers will really hear, understand, believe and obey. Others will be repelled by the gospel message. By their response to Christ in us and in our message, we identify those who are the elect. But the elect are not particular individuals. Rather, they are a general category of those who honestly seek to know truth and will respond with faith and obedience when they hear it.

It may not be possible to bring to repentance some who have left the church and now are unbelievers. It may not be possible to reach others who have never become Christians. It would be a tragic mistake for Churches of Christ to make radical changes in an effort to bring back the former members who are now unbelievers or to attract those who have never obeyed the gospel. Churches of Christ must not be like the politicians who study the latest opinion polls so that they can say what people want to hear. The model must not be those who want to know which way the parade is going so that they can get out in front and lead it. Doing theology by opinion poll is a path that leads to destruction.

## Problems Created by Manipulation

Some preachers who have not understood the biblical doctrine of General Election have used fear and guilt appeals in an effort to motivate more members of the church to be more involved in evangelism. The goal they seek to achieve is good, but their misguided efforts have done more harm than good.

Among the 325 essays from former members who now have left Churches of Christ, at least two dozen complained about feeling manipulated by fear and guilt appeals. Here is what one former member wrote:

> When I was a member of the Church of Christ, I always went home from church feeling depressed, guilty and afraid that the Lord would return when I knew that I was not yet ready for the judgment day. No matter how much I did, I always knew that I could have done more. I now believe that I was being manipulated.

One woman who joined an independent community-type church wrote about how much better she felt after attending worship assemblies at that church. Here is a part of what she said:

> At the church I now attend, we are led in rejoicing. We celebrate the security we have in the grace of God. We occasionally hear Bible lessons that include reproof, rebuke and correction – but most of the emphasis is on the joy we share in Christ.

One man, no longer a member of the Churches of Christ, explained why he left:

> I do not think that I have the gifts for being a soul-winner, but in the Church of Christ I felt condemned because I did not support the preacher's door-knocking approach to evangelism. I never attended the Personal Evangelism Training classes. I never went to a Soul Winning Workshop. I may have influenced a few friends and relatives who later obeyed the gospel. But it was someone else who showed them the Jule Miller filmstrips. I did not know how to do that. But after a while I got tired of being whipped from the pulpit every time I went to church. Now I do not go to church anywhere. I don't feel good about myself, and I know that I will probably go to hell. But at least I am not hurting right now the way I did when I went to the Church of Christ.

I assume that the preacher who drove that man away from the church was acting from good motives. I share his interest in getting all Christians involved in evangelism. But I do not believe that we all have to be involved in the same way. I favor a team approach to evangelism. I do not want to take away any good argument preachers use to encourage more members to be more actively involved in evangelism. But we cannot achieve that objective by using bad arguments to manipulate the members.

Chapter **10**

# The Instrumental Music Issue

The instrumental music issue was mentioned more than any other issue in the "Why I Left Churches of Christ" survey. Out of the 325 who responded, 53 now belong to independent community-type churches and virtually all of these use instrumental music. Exactly the same number, 53, are now members of a Christian church. The most obvious thing that sets these Christian churches apart from Churches of Christ is that they use instrumental music and Churches of Christ, historically, have not.

Congregational singing without the accompaniment of instrumental music is one of the first things that visitors have noticed when they attended worship assemblies of the Churches of Christ. Most churches, Roman Catholic and Protestant, use organs, pianos or other instruments. Sometimes the instrumental music is used alone, without any singing. It may be used as a kind of prelude before the other worship activities begin. It could be used to fill the silence while the offering is collected. It might be used as a recessional at the end of the service. Most often it is used as accompaniment for a choir, or for congregational singing.

The absence of instrumental music has, historically, been characteristic of Churches of Christ, and it still is characteristic of a very large majority of congregations. This practice seems very strange to many people in the United States today. They do not see why it is an issue at all. Within Churches of Christ, however, it is the subject of much discussion. Congregations are dividing over this issue. Several large congregations that historically have been identified with the non-instrumental Churches of Christ have started using instrumental music in at least some of their worship assemblies. In 2003 the Christian Chronicle reported that five Churches of Christ had added instrumental services: Northwest in Seattle, Wash.; Oak Hills in San Antonio, Texas; Farmers Branch in Dallas, Texas; Southlake in Grapevine, Texas; and Amarillo South in Amarillo, Texas. In 2008 the Quail Springs congregation in Oklahoma City added an instrumental service and started using the term "both/and" to describe this arrangement of having one instrumental and one non-instrumental service. Since then other congregations have joined this trend.

By far the largest and most influential congregation to adopt this practice was the Richland Hills Church of Christ (now known as "The Hills Church of Christ") located in a suburb north of Fort Worth, Texas.[1] Rick Atchley, the preacher for this congregation, has become the leading advocate of this arrangement. In December 2006, he had three lessons on "The Both/And Church" that were on the congregation's website and available by recordings that have been widely distributed. In 2006 they were reported to be the largest Church of Christ in the nation.[2] There appears to be a danger of another major rift in this fellowship similar to what happened shortly after the Civil War when Churches of Christ and Christian Churches became two separate groups. For that reason, it seems necessary to devote a full chapter to this issue. The place to start would seem to be with an update and a relatively brief historical review.

## An Update

The February 2012 edition of the *Christian Chronicle* had an article with the headline "Churches with instrumental services return to directory."[3] According to this article, churches that formerly had a cappella worship exclusively – but then added instrumental services – were omitted from the 2009 edition of the directory *Churches of Christ in the United States*. The assumption of the publisher was that when a cappella Churches of Christ started having instrumental services, they essentially became a part of the Christian Churches and Churches of Christ (instrumental).[4]

In the past, whenever heirs of the Restoration Movement changed their position on the instrumental music issue, they left Churches of Christ and joined a Christian church – or they left the Christian church and identified with a Church of Christ. But leaders of those "both/and" congregations expected that most of their members who had been attending lectureships and workshops with the Churches of Christ that still use a cappella music only, would continue to do so. They did not expect that many of their members would attend the North American Christian Convention with the instrumental brethren. They expected that most of their members would keep on sending their children to Christian colleges and universities established and supported by people in the a cappella fellowship. When the directory publisher asked the Richland Hills leaders if they wanted to be listed in the same directory that included all of the a cappella congregations – but with some note showing that they have both a cappella and instrumental services – they said that they did.

News of the directory change on *The Christian Chronicle* blog was met with mixed responses. Some favored including the "both/and" congregations. More were critical of the decision to put those congregations back in the directory. In personal conversations with various church leaders I found more who wanted to keep the directory for a cappella congregations only.

Advocates of the "both/and" arrangement say that they cannot understand why most people in the Churches of Christ object to their practice. They say, "We still have a non-instrumental service and that should be enough to satisfy your conscience. If you don't want a worship service with instrumental music, just go to the a cappella service." But those for whom this is a matter of conscience say that the "both/and" approach is not acceptable. They see it as being like a congregation having one worship service for those who want to observe the Lord's Supper every Sunday and another worship service for those who want to observe the Lord's Supper just once a year. They regard it as being like a congregation that keeps its baptistery for those who prefer immersion, but also installs a "baptismal font" for those who prefer sprinkling – and has one worship service for those who prefer immersion and another for those who prefer sprinkling. Those who do not want the "both/and" churches to be listed in the directory say that doing so makes it more likely that this practice will spread.

## Historical Background

Instrumental music played an important role in the worship assemblies at the tabernacle in the days of Moses and the Exodus. The rituals at the tabernacle and later at the temple were like great musical dramas with several different kinds of musical instruments. On some occasions there were male and female choirs. The rituals involved priests in elaborate ceremonial robes, animal sacrifice, burnt offerings, the sprinkling of blood, holy water, ceremonial lamps and incense.

In the 400 silent years between Malachi and Matthew, the temple still existed, but the focus of Jewish religious life shifted from the temple in Jerusalem to the synagogues which were built in cities throughout the world. The Sabbath assemblies in the synagogues involved Scripture reading, teaching, prayers and chants. But the singing was done without the accompaniment of instrumental music.[5]

The worship assemblies of the early church were quite different from the temple ritual, but very similar to the synagogue assemblies. Singing is one of the things that early Christians did in the Lord's Day assemblies, but there are no New Testament references to instrumental music in Christian worship. The first references to instrumental music in the writings of the early church fathers were not in relation to the worship assemblies. Instead, they were warnings against any use of instrumental music at all. That kind of music was so closely related to the idolatry of pagan rituals, that Christians were warned against it.

There was no church-approved use of instrumental music until A.D. 670 when Pope Vitalian approved of using an organ. But that was only for the imperial court, not for the church.[6] The Latin term *a cappella* literally means "as in the church." In the Pope's private chapel at the Vatican, the singing is still without instrumental accompaniment. It was not until after A.D. 1050 that the use of instrumental music became common in Roman Catholic churches. The Eastern Orthodox Catholic Church continues to use singing without instrumental music.

What was happening in the Roman Catholic Church was that many elements of the tabernacle and temple ritual from the Old Testament were borrowed and made a part of Christian liturgy. Bishops, cardinals and popes wore costumes at least as grand as those of the high priests in the Old Testament. Ordinary priests wore ceremonial robes that set the clergy apart from the laity. They used such things as holy water, incense, and ceremonial candles. And they started using instrumental music. That practice was rejected by Martin Luther, Huldrych Zwingli, John Calvin, John Knox, John Wesley, and other leaders of the Protestant Reformation Movement. They regarded it as a relic of Roman Catholicism. But within just a few generations, instrumental music became common in most Protestant churches.

The Stone-Campbell Restoration Movement began in the United States in the early 1800s. This was a "back-to-the-Bible" effort to reproduce all of the essential elements of what the early church was supposed to be and to do. In this effort, they used a very conservative approach to Bible interpretation. They believed that everything the church does must be biblically authorized. That was the position of Alexander Campbell and other Restoration Movement pioneers. Because of that belief, they opposed any use of instrumental music in congregational worship assemblies.

Throughout the nineteenth century, all of the congregations identified with the Stone-Campbell Restoration Movement were identified as "Christian Churches" in the reference book, *Religious Bodies*, published by the U.S. Census Bureau. Before the Civil War, all of these congregations were a cappella.

In the decades after the Civil War, many of these congregations started using instrumental music. In the 1906 edition of *Religious Bodies,* for the first time, the Census Bureau reported data on the Churches of Christ separate from the report on the Christian Churches. By then it had become clear that these two informal fellowships of independent congregations could be identified as separate bodies. The most obvious difference was that Christian Churches used instrumental music while Churches of Christ did not.

Some of the people who responded to this "Why I Left Churches of Christ" survey said that they had changed their belief on the instrumental music issue. But it does not appear that any of these went to congregations using the "both/and" arrangement. It would be beyond the scope of this book to give an extended discussion of why the churches they left do not use instrumental music. The brief bottom-line explanation is that they believe that there is no authority in the New Testament for using instrumental music in the worship assemblies of the church. Some of those who left still hold that belief, but they decided that this is not a "salvation issue." Others have come to believe that there really is biblical authority for using instrumental music in Christian worship. More, however, have decided that the absence of biblical authorization is not enough to prohibit instrumental music in the church. Here is what one man wrote.

> I grew up hearing that it would be wrong to use instrumental music in worship services of the church, but I have read the entire New Testament, and I do not find any commandment forbidding its use. I finally came to the conclusion that if there is something God does not want me to do, He will have to say so plainly.

This man went to one of the Christian Churches. I wonder if he realizes that their position may be more conservative than his. In the Christian Church (Disciples of Christ) and in most liberal Protestant denominations it is commonly assumed that we can do anything that the Bible does not clearly say we must not do. That approach to Bible interpretation goes back to Luther's view that we should not do anything that the Bible expressly forbids. More conservative denominations of the Reformed Church tradition use Zwingli's rule that we must do only what the Bible mandates. That is what they call the "regulative principle." That was the approach to Bible interpretation used by all of the pioneers of the Stone-Campbell Restoration Movement. It is also the approach to Bible authority used in Rick Atchley's three sermons on "The Both/And Church." Atchley believes that there is Bible authority for instrumental music in worship assemblies.

The regulative principle is still used by most of the independent and conservative Christian Churches just as it is by Churches of Christ. I also wonder if this survey respondent realizes how inappropriate it is for a mere human to tell the Creator and Ruler of the universe how He should make His will known to us.

A few of those who left Churches of Christ over this issue said that they had come to believe that there really is authorization in the New Testament for instrumental music in worship assemblies. But in our survey most of them did not say what that authorization was. The few who did simply repeated arguments that have been made and answered for years. The same thing has been true of the arguments presented by Rick Atchley and other defenders of the "Both/And" approach. They have no new arguments and no new evidence to support their claims.

Every church leader, whether on the instrumental or non-instrumental side of the issue, should carefully study an excellent book by Dr. Thomas C. Alexander, *Music in Worship: A New Examination of an Old Issue*.[7] It is a fair, balanced and thoroughly biblical examination of the arguments made by Atchley and those who agree with him. The book focuses specifically on the question "Does the Bible justify instrumental music for Christian worship?" Tom Alexander is a professor of Bible at Harding University where he has served since 1978. He is a former Dean of Harding's College of Bible and Religion. He also serves as one of the elders of the College Church of Christ in Searcy, Ark. I have known and loved this brother since I came to Harding in 1990. He is well known and respected by members of the Churches of Christ throughout the world. I believe that the following material from the back cover of his 125-page book is worth repeating here.

> In 2006, advocates for the use of instrumental music in worship presented a three-part series titled "The Both/And Church," suggesting that people should read old texts in fresh, new ways. These advocates proposed that their understanding of biblical texts justifies instruments in church worship. Since that time, some churches have followed their lead.
>
> Ironically, this misreading of the relevant biblical texts is not new. The arguments made by these proponents are the arguments that have been made since the late 1800s among advocates of instrumental music in worship.

> Thomas Alexander answers these "new" arguments in a careful, biblical way in *Music in Worship*. He carefully evaluates each of the reasons given by "both/and church" proponents and shows that the facts about what God wants in worship have not changed – human attitudes have.

The 20 pages of notes at the end of Alexander's book are filled with documentation of what the advocates of the "both/and" approach have said along with references to many useful books.[8] There is nothing that I could add to what has already been written. My purpose in this report of survey results is simply to focus on why these people left Churches of Christ and respond to what they said where it seems appropriate – especially in regard to the present situation and future trends.

## What Is Wrong With Asking, "Is This a Salvation Issue?"

Many of those who responded to this survey expressed the belief that the instrumental music question is not a "salvation issue." I do not think that they mean that it is not an issue dealing with how we are saved. By the term "salvation issue" I think that they mean that it an issue that one does not have to get right in order to make it to heaven. Among those of us who have not left Churches of Christ, there may be a few who are sure that this really is an issue that you have to get right in order to be saved. More, in my opinion, share the belief that it is not appropriate for us to make lists of the salvation issues.

I understand that Bible doctrines are not all of equal importance. When Jesus was asked "What is the greatest commandment?" He did not respond by saying "All 613 statutes that the Rabbis have identified in the Law of Moses are of equal importance." Instead He identified two commandments that, together, are the most important: Love God with all your soul, mind, heart and strength, and Love your neighbor as yourself (Mark 12:28-31). Jesus condemned the Pharisees who were careful to give a tithe of the herbs grown in their gardens, but they neglected the "weightier matters of the law; justice and mercy and faithfulness." Jesus called them "blind guide, straining out a gnat but swallowing a camel" (Matthew 23:23-24). Consider what the apostle Paul told the Christians in Corinth:

> For I delivered to you as of first importance what I also received: that Christ died for our sins in accordance with the Scriptures, that he was buried, that he was raised on the third day in accordance with the Scriptures, and that he appeared to Cephas, then to the twelve. Then he appeared to more than five hundred brothers at one time, most of whom are still alive, though some have fallen asleep. Then he appeared to James, then to all the apostles. Last of all, as to one untimely born, he appeared also to me. (1 Corinthians 15:3-8)

Some things are "of first importance." Other things are of lesser importance.

Consider also what the writer of Hebrews said about the need to move on from the milk to the meat of God's Word – to leave the elementary teachings and go on to maturity (Hebrews 5:11–6:3). Some Bible doctrines, obviously, are more important than others. Not all commands have equal priority. But when people argue about whether the instrumental music question is a "salvation issue," they are making two fundamental errors.

The first of these errors is that this is what a debater would call a red herring. The real issue in this context is the question "Does the Bible justify instrumental music for Christian worship?" The question is not the relative importance of this issue. One might grant that there are many far more important issues without regarding this as an issue that can be ignored. When Jesus identified two commandments that, together, had the highest priority, He did not imply that all of the other commandments could be ignored.[9] Jesus did not condemn the Pharisees for giving a tithe of the herbs from their gardens. He said, "These you ought to have done, without neglecting the others." Jesus did not condemn the Pharisees for "straining out a gnat." If you find a gnat floating around in your drink, it would be a good idea to strain it out. Swallowing a camel, however, would be far worse – if it were possible. When Paul called the death, burial, resurrection and appearances of Christ matters of "first importance," he did not say to neglect everything else. When the writer of Hebrews said to go on from the milk to the meat of God's Word, he did not mean that we ever outgrow our need for that milk.

If a person wants to argue about the relative importance of various Bible doctrines and commands, that is a totally different subject. Perhaps those who bring up the so-called "salvation issue" here are not fully aware of what they are doing. What they are doing is distracting the discussion from the topic at hand. Their argument does not help Christians get closer to God's will on this matter.

The second fundamental problem is that arguing about whether something is a "salvation issue" reflects a serious misunderstanding of what the Bible teaches about salvation. I have seen several different lists of these so-called "salvation issues" and no two of them fully agree. All of them, however, are built on the same false premise. The term "salvation issue" implies that these are the issues that people must understand in order to get to heaven. But the Bible does not teach that our eternal salvation is based on our correct understanding of various Bible doctrines. The Bible teaches that we are saved by grace through faith – and not by works (Ephesians 2:8-9). No matter how much we learn and how many good works we perform, we can never be worthy of salvation. I know that I have said this before, but I need to repeat it here: If we had to perfectly understand all doctrinal issues in order to go to heaven, there would be no hope for any of us. And if we had to obey all commands perfectly in order to have eternal salvation, no one could be saved.

This was the big issue between Martin Luther and the Roman Catholic Church. The Catholic position was that our salvation is based, in part, on our good works. Luther taught that the basis of salvation was grace on God's part and faith on our part. The Lutheran and Catholic positions both recognized the importance of grace, faith and good works. The difference was in what the two views saw as the basis of salvation. Leaders of the Protestant Reformation Movement disagreed on many matters, but they all shared the view that God's grace is the only basis of salvation. They also shared the understanding that it is only our faith that God counts for righteousness. Our good works are important, but our works are never perfect and therefore they cannot be the basis of our salvation. Pioneers of the Stone-Campbell Restoration Movement shared this understanding. They put more emphasis on obedience – especially in regard to baptism – than most Protestant denominations. But when they taught that baptism for the forgiveness of sins is essential to salvation, they did not regard baptism as a work of merit. They saw baptism simply as a work of obedience.

The instrumental music question is not as important as many other doctrines, but no doctrine or practice is really a "salvation issue." Instead of being distracted by an argument over what is and what is not a "salvation issue," we should focus on the real issue: Does the Bible authorize the use of instrumental music in the worship assemblies of the Lord's church? If a careful study using all the principles of good Bible scholarship shows that it does, then we should no longer object to its use. But if that study does not show biblical justification for this practice, then we should not use instrumental music in Christian worship.

## An Examination of Alternatives

There are many factors to consider when leaving one congregation and joining another. What a congregation does about using or not using instrumental music is not the only factor to consider. It is not the most important thing. But it is one thing that a faithful Christian ought to consider. If someone is a member of a congregation that uses instrumental music and their careful study brings them to the conclusion that this practice has no biblical authorization, they have two possible options. One of these alternatives is to recognize that no congregation is perfect. If you ever found a perfect congregation and joined it, that congregation would then no longer be perfect because you are not perfect. One might, therefore, decide to remain in an instrumental congregation despite its error on this one point. A serious problem with that alternative, however, is that the use of instrumental music is so much a part of a congregation's shared experience that it is impossible to ignore. It would also involve your influence. Participating with others in an activity does not necessarily imply approval of all the others with whom you share in that activity. But it would seem rather clearly to imply approval of the activity.

There is another alternative for those who are members of congregations that uses instrumental music and who have decided that this practice has no biblical authorization. They can leave those congregations and affiliate with non-instrumental congregations. They certainly have the right and the responsibility to tell others why they are leaving. But this should be as an explanation, not as an attack. It should be done in a spirit of humility and gentleness. It should be an invitation to dialogue, not a challenge to debate. The decision to leave such a congregation should be based on your personal conscience and convictions, not on a judgment that those who disagree with you will not go to heaven.

There is a very serious warning that should be considered. It clearly would be wrong to remain in a congregation in order to participate in a clandestine movement – an underground effort seeking to overthrow the leaders, fire the ministers, and transition that instrumental church into one that is non-instrumental. That is similar to what happened in many Christian Churches in the first half of the 20th century. People who had a hidden agenda came into very conservative congregations of the Christian Churches and gradually transitioned them into more liberal churches. The "open membership" practice started in foreign missions but gradually spread to Christian Churches in the United States. They accepted into their congregations, on a simple transfer of membership, people who had never been immersed as believers. This hidden agenda also involved having Christian Churches participate in the National or World Council of Churches where most of the participating denominations were very liberal in their theology. Gradually, theological liberalism spread into the Christian Churches. These leaders of the Christian Churches became more and more involved in the Ecumenical Movement and its effort to achieve church union by merging denominational structures. The last straw for many was when these leaders of the Christian Churches decided that they could not participate fully in this so-called "unity movement" until they created a central denominational headquarters that could speak for all the Christian Churches. That was what was involved in the "Restructure" plan of the 1950s.[10]

Most members of the Churches of Christ are unaware of the history of what happened to transition very conservative Christian Churches into the far more liberal Christian Church (Disciples of Christ). There are, however, some very good histories of this period.[11] Members of the Churches of Christ are more likely to have heard about what happened in the late 19th century when congregations that had always opposed the use of instrumental music in Christian worship were transitioned into Christian Churches. By 1906, a majority of the congregations had adopted the instrumental position. Many congregations that had previously been non-instrumental were taken over by those who favored instrumental music. Most of the church buildings that had been built and paid for by non-instrumental people were then owned by the instrumental brethren. The non-instrumental people had to leave and start over. All but one of the colleges built by Restoration Movement heirs were taken over by those who defended the use of instrumental music in worship assemblies.

My master's thesis was a study of one reason the Restoration Movement heirs divided over some issues but managed to differ without dividing over others.[12] This movement was much more likely to divide over very obvious things that were a part of a congregation's shared experience – like instrumental music in the assembly – than over privately held beliefs. But the rhetorical strategies used by movement leaders also played an important role. The debate approach often led to division. The dialogue approach helped build consensus.

This history should be studied carefully by those who leave a non-instrumental congregation and go to an instrumental congregation. Those who are not familiar with this history are much more likely to repeat it. Among those who left Churches of Christ in this study, one-third either went to the Christian Churches or to an independent community-type congregation. None of them went to one of the Churches of Christ that now have one instrumental and one non-instrumental worship assembly. Many of the preachers for those "both/and" congregations have expressed their goal of transitioning many congregations and eventually this whole fellowship. They say that they want all Churches of Christ to either start using instrumental music, or at least to stop saying that instrumental music should not be used in Christian worship. From a social movement perspective, their strategy appears to be one of infiltration and subversion.

There is an obvious parallel in the history of Pentecostalism. Oral Roberts urged his followers not to leave their mainstream denominations. He told them not to form a new denomination. He said that they should not join an existing Pentecostal denomination. Instead, he said that they should stay in their mainstream denominations and spread their beliefs in such things as tongue-speaking, miraculous healing, and exorcism. Roberts, who had belonged to an old-line Pentecostal denomination, joined the Boston Avenue Methodist Church in Tulsa, Okla. This effort to infiltrate mainstream denominations with charismatic beliefs and practices had some degree of success. Some congregations of the Christian Churches and the Christian Church (Disciples of Christ) were taken over by charismatics. Despite the efforts by Pat Boone and a few others, the effort to infiltrate Churches of Christ met with very little success.

There are major questions about the ethics of the infiltration and subversion strategies. These questions should be considered very carefully by people moving from instrumental to non-instrumental congregations and by those moving from non-instrumental to instrumental congregations.

Some have come to the conclusion that it makes no difference whether a congregation uses or does not use instrumental music. There are more alternatives available to them. Singing is a part of the worship assembly in both instrumental and non-instrumental congregations. There are people who are equally comfortable in either. They can worship with or without instrumental accompaniment. If they are or become members of a historically non-instrumental congregation, they need to hold their position on this matter as a privately held belief. They must not try to transition that church into an instrumental congregation. It would be better for them to leave and affiliate with a congregation that already uses instrumental music.

## Conclusion

At least one generation has grown up in Churches of Christ without a clear understanding of the instrumental music issue. They know that Churches of Christ, historically, have not used instrumental music in the worship assemblies, but they have not really understood why. Some have heard an argument based on the Greek word *psallo* as though it were something new. They are not familiar with the way that argument has been answered over and over again for more than 100 years. Some have heard that the use of instrumental music in the Old Testament worship at the tabernacle and temple justifies the use of instrumental music in Christian worship. They think that this argument is something fresh and new. They have not been taught enough about correct biblical interpretation to understand why these Old Testament examples do not apply in the church. The same thing is true in regard to arguments based on highly figurative references in Revelation to instrumental music in heaven. Some have assumed that the absence of clear instructions forbidding the use of instrumental music in the worship assemblies justifies its use. They have not had enough instruction about hermeneutics so that they understand why that assumption involves a radical shift away from a very solid foundation to one that is much more permissive. I am not suggesting that this topic become a major theme in sermons, but it could at least be mentioned occasionally. Bible classes would be a much better context for serious study of Bible interpretation.

Christian parents have the right to expect something when they send their children to a college or university established and supported by members of the Churches of Christ. They certainly have the right to expect that school to reinforce the things taught in their homes and local congregations. It was, therefore, with deep regret that I learned about Abilene Christian University now having both a cappella chapel Monday-Wednesday-Friday and instrumental music in some of their small group chapels on Tuesday and Thursday. During the chapel part of their opening convocation last August, the band played while the congregation sang the Doxology.[13]

One of the major challenges in this matter is that recent generations have had less and less ability to follow closely reasoned arguments. Most political campaigns are won or lost based on slogans and sound bites rather than on serious discussion of the issues. In a similar way, many people have become content with "bumper sticker" theology. They are more likely to base decisions on their feelings than on reason. But church leaders are capable of meeting this challenge, if only they will try. Future generations must learn that the final authority is what the Bible teaches and not what they feel or think. "I see nothing wrong with it" does not settle the matter.

Chapter **11**

# The Role of Women

Seven women who used this survey to explain why they left Churches of Christ said that their main objection to Churches of Christ was its doctrine concerning the role of women. Here is what one of them wrote:

> I grew up in Churches of Christ, but I left because I felt stifled by an oppressive atmosphere of male chauvinism. I have a good education. I believe that I have God-given gifts of leadership, and those gifts are recognized in the business world – but not in Churches of Christ. I was allowed to teach a Ladies' Bible class and often was called upon to speak at retreats for women. In the Sunday morning Bible classes, I was permitted to teach children. But as soon as any of the boys were old enough to be baptized, I could not teach them any longer. I know how to do strategic planning, but I was never asked to serve on any of the congregation's committees. I am not a radical feminist, but I believe that many of the rules about what women are not permitted to do are just traditions based on a doctrine of male superiority. When I

> finally left Churches of Christ, I joined a community church where I have felt free to use my God-given gifts.

The following is what another one of these women said:

> I am a special education teacher at one of the public schools in [name of city omitted]. I teach both deaf and hearing students. The Church of Christ that I attended had a ministry to the deaf. I was often asked to translate the sermons, songs and prayers into sign language. The deaf and hearing-impaired members sat on the front few rows of seats on one side of the auditorium. Women were allowed to sign for the deaf, but only from a seated position. Women who were fluent in Spanish were not allowed to translate because that would require speaking out loud. Women were not asked to serve as ushers or greeters. I never had a burning desire to pass the communion trays, but I never could understand why that had to be a male-only role. It also bothered me that the young boys and girls from that congregation participated in a training program called "Lads to Leaders and Lasses to Leaderettes." That "ettes" ending is demeaning for females. It suggests that females can never really be leaders – just a smaller version of leaders. Young girls who participated in activities involving public speaking could practice at home with help from fathers. But in the actual competition, fathers were not allowed in the same room where their daughters were speaking. Eventually I got fed up with all of these man-made rules. I joined a denomination where women are allowed to play a much more important role.

Another one of these comments is worth including here:

> Some of the most meaningful prayers I ever heard were spoken by women in a class for women only. But the elders in the Church of Christ where I grew up had a rule against a woman "leading" a prayer if any males were present. Frankly, I never could understand why praying to God in an audible voice was a leadership role reserved for men only.

> The congregation that I attended had small group meetings in homes. In one of those small group meetings someone suggested that we stand in a circle holding hands and have a chain prayer. I spoke one of those prayers, and I was summoned before the entire eldership. They ordered me never to do that again. That is when and why I left.

There are Churches of Christ where one still finds this kind of atmosphere, but I do not believe that it is typical of Churches of Christ. Radical feminists, however, have a distorted view of what most conservative religious groups teach. The Southern Baptist Convention recently reaffirmed a belief statement that included this language: "Wives should submit to the servant leadership of their husbands." The liberal media ridiculed the Baptists. They painted them as being male chauvinists from the Stone Age. Churches of Christ are similar to the Baptists and other conservative religious groups in that they all believe the Bible teaches a doctrine of male spiritual leadership that is servant leadership.

## Roles of Men and Women in the Home

My personal understanding is that the Bible teaches that men and women are equal in the sight of God; but men and women are different, and they have roles that complement each other. Male-female difference and their complementary roles go back to the creation (Genesis 1:26-27). Both men and women are created in the image of God. Everything good about masculinity and femininity comes from the nature of God. God formed Adam, the first human, "of dust from the ground and breathed into his nostrils the breath of life" (2:7). But God said, "It is not good that the man should be alone; I will make him a helper fit for him" (v. 18). God made Eve, the first woman, out of a rib taken from Adam's side. That had important symbolic meaning as noted in Chapter 7. Eve was not made out of a bone taken from Adam's foot, as though he should walk over her. The bone from which she was made was not taken from Adam's head, as though she should walk over him. She was made from a bone taken out of Adam's side, from under his arm. The symbolic meaning was that they should walk through life together as equals with Adam protecting Eve while she functioned as a suitable helper for Adam.

The order and events of creation had symbolic meaning as an archetypal image. Adam was created first, then Eve. Eve was created as a helper suitable for Adam. Eve was deceived and was the first to sin. Because of the sin of Adam and Eve, a curse was placed on fallen mankind. Adam was told, "[C]ursed is the ground because of you; in pain you shall eat of it all the days of your life; thorns and thistles it shall bring forth for you; and you shall eat the plants of the field. By the sweat of your face you shall eat bread, till you return to the ground, for out of it you were taken; for you are dust, and to dust you shall return" (Genesis 3:17-19). Eve was told, "I will surely multiply your pain in childbearing; in pain you shall bring forth children. Your desire shall be for your husband, and he shall rule over you" (v. 16).

In 1 Timothy 2:13-14, Paul used this archetypal image as support for an argument. "For Adam was formed first, then Eve; and Adam was not deceived, but the woman was deceived and became a transgressor." In this passage, Paul uses the order and events of creation as the basis for his claim to "[l]et a woman learn quietly with all submissiveness. I do not permit a woman to teach or to exercise authority over a man; rather, she is to remain quiet" (vv. 11-12). This is said in the context of a letter in which Paul told Timothy what was needed at the church in Ephesus. A part of that involved the roles of men and women. Paul wrote, "I desire then that in every place the men should pray, lifting holy hands without anger or quarreling" (v. 8). Then in the next two verses, Paul focused on how women should dress. And in verses 11-12, he gave instruction about the roles of men and women. Some people today have tried to explain Paul's language as an adaptation to first-century culture in places like Ephesus. But the basis of Paul's instruction about women not being in positions of authority as teachers over men in the church is the order and events of creation, not first-century culture in Ephesus.

In 1 Peter 3:1-7 Peter used the archetypal image of Sarah in urging Christian wives to submit to their husbands, to be pure and reverent and to focus on inner beauty, "For this is the way the holy women of the past who put their hope in God used to make themselves beautiful" (v. 5 NIV1984). Peter held up Sarah as an example and wrote, "You are her daughters if you do what is right and do not give way to fear"

(v. 6 NIV1984). Elsewhere the model of submission goes back to Eve in the Garden of Eden (Genesis 3:16). Eve was the prototype – the first model. Many faithful daughters of Eve (and of Sarah) have followed that same example.

First Peter 3:7 is often misunderstood. Husbands are told to be "considerate" toward their wives and to treat them with respect as "the weaker partner" (NIV1984). The English Standard and New King James Versions have a more literal translation: "the weaker vessel." Greek scholars tell us that the reference here is to the more delicate vessels used for a meal – the fine china and the delicate crystal. The contrast is with men as the ordinary clay pots – stronger in some ways, but not as special.

Are women the "weaker sex"? In terms of brute force, the average man is larger and stronger than the average woman. But women live about 5 to 10 years longer than men. Women are more resistant to disease, and they tolerate pain better. This passage should never be used to support a doctrine of male superiority.

In Ephesians 5:22-24, Paul wrote, "Wives, submit to your own husbands, as to the Lord. For the husband is the head of the wife even as Christ is the head of the church, his body, and is himself its Savior. Now as the church submits to Christ, so also wives should submit in everything to their husbands." It is important to notice that verse 22 does not have a verb in the original Greek text. It is just "Wives, to husbands as to the Lord." To fill in the blank, one has to go back to verse 21, "submitting to one another out of reverence for Christ." A participle gets its force from a commanding verb elsewhere in the sentence – usually earlier in the sentence. But verses 19-20 also have participles instead of verbs: "addressing one another in psalms and hymns and spiritual songs, singing and making melody to the Lord with your heart, giving thanks always and for everything to God the Father in the name of our Lord Jesus Christ." The commanding verb is in verse 18, "And do not get drunk with wine, for that is debauchery, but be filled with the [Holy] Spirit." The participles show what you do when you are filled with the Holy Spirit. You will be speaking to one another in psalms, hymns and spiritual songs; singing and making melody with your heart; giving thanks for everything; and submitting to one another out of reverence for Christ (vv. 19-21).

Under the general heading of "submitting to one another out of reverence for Christ," the first section is about wives submitting to husbands. But that is not the last of these sections. The next is addressed to husbands, and it is much longer. In Ephesians 5:25-33, Paul began with the instructions, "Husbands, love your wives, as Christ loved the church and gave himself up for her" (v. 25). Then he said, "In the same way husbands should love their wives as their own bodies. He who loves his wife loves himself" (v. 28). And he concluded by saying, "[L]et each one of you love his wife as himself, and let the wife see that she respects her husband" (v. 33).

The command for husbands to love their wives "as Christ loved the church" (Ephesians 5:25) had important implications. Jesus is Lord, but Jesus did not say, "Church, you die for me." Instead he said, "I will die for you." A husband should love his wife enough to die for her. If a husband is a servant leader, he will put his wife's needs ahead of his own. Husbands and wives should seek to outdo each other in giving love, showing affection and giving service. Each should do what is best for the other. I believe that in the home as God would have it to be, most decisions are made by consensus. The husband and wife discuss things until they come to an agreement on what they will do. But there will be times when each wants to do what is best for the other, and they cannot agree. That, I believe, is when the husband as the spiritual leader of the family breaks the tie by deciding to do what is best for the wife.

As I write this chapter, my wife and I have just recently celebrated our 57th wedding anniversary. I was a church-supported minister for 20 of those years and then a university professor for 37 years. Often, as frequently happens with preachers and professors, there was too much month left at the end of the money. Sometimes we did not agree on what to do with our limited funds. My wife might say that I really needed to buy a new suit because my old blue serge suit was getting so worn that she was embarrassed to see me wear it when I preached. I might reply that a greater need was for her to get a new dress because it had been so long since she had bought a new dress. Usually we could reach consensus, and I would get the new suit or she would get the new dress. At times, however, we could not agree. That was when I had to break the tie and make the decision; she would get the dress. The decision of servant leaders should not be to do what is in their best interest. It must be to do what is in the best interest of the wife. The decision is not about who gets his or her way. Rather it is about who gets to sacrifice to do what is in the best interest of the other. Contrary to what the radical feminist may say, it is not hard or demeaning for a wife to submit to that kind of servant leadership.

Actually, what usually happened was that I did not get the suit and my wife did not get the new dress because the children needed shoes and many other things. Children are told to obey their parents, but parents are told to put the needs of their children ahead of their own. That is what love does. Parents are in positions of power and authority over children, but it is not about power or authority. It is about service. Some have claimed that women cannot be equal to men if they submit to the leadership of men – even to servant leadership. They claim that submission implies inferiority. But none of those who take this position have answered the argument about the voluntary submission of God's Son to the Father. In Philippians Paul clearly teaches that Jesus Christ, God the Son, was equal in every way to God the Father. But God the Son voluntarily submitted to God the Father:

> Have this mind among yourselves, which is yours in Christ Jesus, who, though he was in the form of God, did not count equality with God a thing to be grasped, but made himself nothing, taking the form of a servant, being born in the likeness of men. And being found in human form, he humbled himself by becoming obedient to the point of death, even death on a cross (Philippians 2:5-8).

If the voluntary submission of God the Son to God the Father did not imply inferiority, then the voluntary submission of Christian women to men in the home and in the church could not imply inferiority. Indeed, one might argue that in this voluntary submission, Christian women more closely resemble Jesus Christ than the male servant leaders ever could.

This might explain a difficult passage in 1 Timothy 2:15 where "she will be saved through childbearing." Obviously, this cannot mean that a woman must give birth to be saved from the guilt, the power and the eternal consequences of sin. In a note on this passage in the NIV Study Bible, there is a list of the three ways this passage has been understood: (1) It speaks of the godly woman finding fulfillment in her role as wife and mother in the home; (2) It refers to women being saved spiritually through the most significant birth of all, the incarnation of Christ; or (3) It refers to women being kept physically safe in childbirth. Some commentators have suggested that 1 Timothy 2:9-14 might cause some women to be depressed because of their submissive role. According to this understanding, verse 15 would mean that women could be saved from despair by the knowledge that in their voluntary submission to a husband in the home and male leaders in the church they reach the highest level humanly possible of reflecting the voluntary submission of Jesus Christ to God the Father.

## Roles of Men and Women in the Church

The only verse that some people consider on this subject is the opening phrase of 1 Corinthians 14:34, "[T]he women should keep silent in the churches." But remember that text without context is pretext. So we need to consider the context.

The immediate context of this passage is the worship assembly when "the whole church comes together" (1 Corinthians 14:23). The subject of 1 Corinthians 11-14 is conduct in the worship assembly: how to observe the Lord's Supper and how to use the miraculous gifts of tongues and prophecy. Just before the verse in question, Paul had given instructions in verses 26-33 to correct disorderly conduct in the assembly.

From 1 Corinthians 14:26, it appears that the assembly at the church in Corinth was very spontaneous: "[E]ach one has a hymn, a lesson, a revelation, a tongue, or an interpretation." Such a spontaneous assembly would be acceptable, but it appears that some were more interested in doing their own thing than in edifying the church. Paul tells them, "Let all things be done for building up" (v. 26).

From 1 Corinthians 14:27-28 it appears that too many Corinthians were speaking in tongues; they were all speaking at the same time; and no one was interpreting. Paul tells them that: there should be no more than two or three speaking in tongues in one assembly; they should take turns; and no one should speak in tongues without an interpreter.

From 1 Corinthians 14:29-33 it appears that: too many prophets were speaking in the Corinthian assembly; other prophets were not listening; prophets were interrupting one another; and some were justifying their disorderly conduct by claiming that they had no power to control their speaking because they were inspired by the Holy Spirit. Paul corrects this by telling them that they should have no more than two or three prophets speaking in one assembly; the prophets should listen to one another; a prophet who is speaking should yield the floor to a prophet who has just received a revelation; and the prophets can control their behavior – even though they are inspired by the Holy Spirit.

From the first part of 1 Corinthians 14:33, it is clear that this discussion was intended to correct disorderly conduct in the assembly: "For God is not a God of confusion but of peace."

The sentence that we are studying in 1 Corinthians 14:34 actually begins in the last part of verse 33, "As in all the churches of the saints, the women should keep silent in the churches." Obviously this instruction was not just for the church in Corinth. But what does it mean? No one interprets "keep silent" to mean that women could not sing in the worship assembly. There is strong support in the New Testament for congregational singing done by both men and women.

## How Does the Text Limit the Meaning of "Keep Silent"?

The next part of 1 Corinthians 14:34 says, "[T]hey are not permitted to speak." The Greek word used here for "speak" is used elsewhere for preaching in "speaking with authority." But it is not always used in that way. So that does not give us a clear answer, and we must continue the study.

The last part of 1 Corinthians 14:34 says that they "should be in submission, as the Law also says." But the Law did not specifically say that women were not permitted to speak in an assembly or even that they must be in submission. Most New Testament scholars think that this is a reference to Genesis 3:16 where Eve was told that Adam would rule over her and that established a pattern for all their descendants.

Based on the order and events of creation and the teaching of

Genesis 3:16, there is a general principle of male spiritual leadership taught throughout the Old Testament and repeated in the New Testament. Women, therefore, were not to speak in the assembly in such a way as to violate the principle of male spiritual leadership.

In addition to studying the context before 1 Corinthians 14:34, we should also consider what came after. Verse 35 says, "If there is anything they desire to learn, let them ask their husbands at home. For it is shameful for a woman to speak in church." Some have concluded that this teaching was addressed to the wives of the prophets who were interrupting their husbands and arguing with them about their prophecies. It is true that the Greek word for "woman" is the same as the word for "wife." This was similar to American hill country dialect in which a man might say "This is my woman" or a woman might say "This is my man," when the references were to a wife or a husband. The translation from the Greek depends on the context. But no version of the English Bible that I have ever seen has "wives" instead of "women" in verse 34.

## How the Doctrine of Male Spiritual Leadership Is Taught

- It is implied in the archetypal image of Eve being told that Adam would rule over her.
- Men were the priests in the Patriarchal dispensation (and there was no Matriarchal age).
- All of the priests at the tabernacle and temple were males.
- All of the apostles in the New Testament were males.
- All of the sermons recorded in the New Testament were preached by males.
- The elders/overseers/shepherds in the New Testament church were husbands and fathers.

Note that in 1 Corinthians 11:2-16, 14:34, and 1 Timothy 2:11-14 the differences between the roles for men and women were justified by the order and events of creation and not accommodations to culture. But because "the women … should be in submission, as the Law also says" (1 Corinthians 14:34), we need to review what women did under the Law – and consider what they did in the New Testament.

- Exodus 15:20: Miriam, the sister of Moses and Aaron was called a prophetess. She "took a tambourine in her hand, and all the women went out after her with tambourines and dancing. And Miriam sang to them: 'Sing to the LORD, for he has triumphed gloriously; the horse and his rider he has thrown into the sea.' " This song was composed by a woman, and that song became a part of Old Testament Scripture.
- Numbers 12:1-2: Miriam claimed that God had spoken through her.
- Judges 4:4: Deborah was a judge and a prophetess – one who delivered the word of God.
- 2 Kings 22:14-20: Huldah was called a prophetess. She delivered the word of God to King Josiah.
- Isaiah 8:3: The wife of Isaiah was called a prophetess.
- Luke 2:26: Anna was called a prophetess, and she spoke "of him [Jesus] to all who were waiting for the redemption of Jerusalem."
- Acts 2:17: Peter quotes the prophecy of Joel that "your sons and your daughters shall prophesy."
- Acts 21:9: Philip, the evangelist, "had four unmarried daughters, who prophesied."
- 1 Corinthians 11:5-16 appears to be about how women in the Corinthian church were to dress in the assembly when they prayed or prophesied. In the New International Version, 1984, the heading at the beginning of chapter 11 is "Propriety in Worship." Some New Testament scholars, however, believe that the assembly part of this chapter does not begin until verse 17 where the instructions are given about the observance of the Lord's Supper. But that view certainly is not where the assembly context appears to begin.
- Romans 16:1: Phoebe was called "a servant of the church in Cenchreae." The Greek text uses the ordinary word for "deacon" – and not "deaconess," a feminine version of that word.
- Romans 16:3: Priscilla is listed before her husband, Aquila, as she often was – for example when and she and her husband taught Apollos about Christ.

Consider also the worthy woman of Proverbs 31. The idea that women are inferior to men and should be kept barefoot and pregnant was not reflected in this passage. Notice the things that this "excellent wife" (v. 10) did.

- Proverbs 31:13-15: "She seeks wool and flax, and works with willing hands. She is like the ships of the merchant; she brings her food from afar. She rises while it is yet night and provides food for her household and portions for her maidens." But her work was not all that of a homemaker.
- Proverbs 31:16: "She considers a field and buys it; with the fruit of her hands she plants a vineyard."
- Proverbs 31:18: "She perceives that her merchandise is profitable."
- Proverbs 31:24: "She makes linen garments and sells them; she delivers sashes to the merchant."
- Proverbs 31:26-31: "She opens her mouth with wisdom, and the teaching of kindness is on her tongue. She looks well to the ways of her household and does not eat the bread of idleness. Her children rise up and call her blessed; her husband also, and he praises her: 'Many women have done excellently, but you surpass them all.' Charm is deceitful, and beauty is vain, but a woman who fears the LORD is to be praised. Give her of the fruit of her hands, and let her works praise her in the gates."

## Conclusion

There are two fundamental Bible doctrines on this subject that must not be compromised. The first of these is that men and women are equal but different. They have different roles, yet roles that are complementary. The second is that men are to be the servant leaders and women are to be in supportive helping roles. How these two Bible doctrines are applied may differ from one culture to another or from one period of history to another. The challenge for Christians is to understand what things are matters of culture, custom, tradition or opinion. Diversity must be allowed in those areas. The fundamental Bible principles, however, must not be denied.

I have conducted some survey research in Churches of Christ throughout the nation asking members how strongly they agree or disagree with various attitude statements. In some of the congregations where I have done this research, church leaders wanted to know the opinion of the members regarding the role of women. I always try to remind church members that we do not do theology by opinion poll. We do theology by careful Bible study. But there are times when church leaders need to know what opinions need to be corrected. In the study regarding the role of women in the church, members of the Churches of Christ have disagreed most strongly with the statement, "Women should serve as elders of the church." Close to that, the next highest level of disagreement has been to the statement that "Women should preach in the worship assemblies." I find it interesting that in liberal Protestant denominations that ordain women as ministers, it is usually in a supporting role rather than as the senior pastor or pulpit minister. The opposition to women serving as elders or to women preaching in the worship assembly are areas where I not only agree that this would not be wise, I personally regard those as two things that would violate fundamental Bible teaching regarding the role of women. For me, this is a matter of conscience – not just of personal opinion.

Some congregations of the Christian Church (Disciples of Christ) have women elders and even teenage elders so that all segments of the congregation will be represented. In that practice they are similar to many liberal Protestant denominations. But that seems to me to be a clear violation of the instructions in 1 Timothy 3:1-7 and Titus 1:5-9 concerning qualifications for elders. Some congregations of the Christian Church (Disciples of Christ) and of various denominations also have women preachers. Many Churches of Christ are studying this issue to be sure that their opposition to women preachers is based on solid Bible scholarship and not just tradition. But I believe that very few Churches of Christ will change on this matter.

Peter gave these instructions to Christian women married to unbelievers. "[W]ives, be subject to your own husbands, so that even if some do not obey the word, they may be won without a word by the conduct of their wives" (1 Peter 3:1). A Christian woman married to an unbeliever faces some major challenges. Her husband does not share what is most important in her life. Her husband will not join with her in prayer. That makes it hard for her to remain faithful to the Lord. But it can be done. In almost every congregation of the Churches of Christ there are faithful Christian men who were won over by the behavior of their wives. Unfortunately, it does not happen that way very often.

In the effort to bring up children in the faith, it helps if the functionally single mother can find godly Christian men – Bible class teachers, youth ministers, or others – to be male spiritual role models for her children. She should help her children participate in area-wide training programs for young people. Send them to Christian camps. She should do everything she can to send her children to a Christian school, if one is available, and send them to a Christian college or university. If that is not possible and they attend a public institution, she should help them select one where there is a strong congregation of the Churches of Christ near the campus and an active campus ministry. Then she should do her best to persuade them to become actively involved with a local congregation and a campus ministry while they are in school.

That will not make up for the lack of a male Christian role model in the home, but it will help.

Chapter 12

# Lessons From Listening

Church leaders can learn many things from exit interviews with members who leave. Those are not very comfortable conversations. The people who have left may be very defensive. Some may be angry and bitter. The tension can be reduced by assuring them that you simply want to know why they left, what their church affiliation is now, and what advice they might have to help church leaders do a better job of ministering to those who have not left. Genuine listening can be therapeutic for those who have left and instructive for the church leaders. Their reasons for leaving Churches of Christ may not be the same as those identified in this study. But some value will be derived from considering seriously the things said by former members as reported in this book.

In some congregations, many new converts seem to drop out of the church within a few months after their conversion. When a congregation has a very low retention rate in regard to adult converts, there may be several reasons. I once did a congregational assessment for a church in which the preacher had done virtually all of the personal evangelism. Throughout the years, he had baptized more than 100 people. But every one of these new converts left that congregation and left Churches of Christ within a few months after their baptism. A part of the problem seemed to be in the kind of evangelism the preacher was doing. But that was not the only factor. The members of that congregation were not doing a good job of assimilating the new converts. When churches do not welcome the new converts, help them make friends in the congregation and get them involved in some area of ministry – those new converts are not likely to stay in the church. The same thing is true with those added to the congregation by a transfer of membership. Those who are not quickly assimilated into the congregation are very likely to "slip through the cracks."

In this chapter, I want to discuss some things churches can do to "close the back door." I want to start with some comments on overcoming negative images. That is usually thought of as something that is needed to make converts. We have to bring new converts in through the front door before they can slip out the back door. In this study, those negative images were given as reasons former members gave for leaving Churches of Christ.

## Overcoming Negative Images

Many of the negative images concerning Churches of Christ are not really accurate – at least they do not apply to a large majority of "mainstream" Churches of Christ. But in some cases these negative images accurately reflect what some individuals and some congregations believe and teach. Therefore, the first step in overcoming negative images is to examine honestly what your congregation teaches and what your members believe. Sometimes we must correct errors within the church before we can reach others with the gospel message. But if the negative images do not accurately reflect what members of your congregation believe, there are things that can be done to communicate your beliefs more effectively.

*"We Think That We Are the Only Ones Going to Heaven"*

Is your congregation located in an area where this is what people believe about Churches of Christ? If so, is that true concerning members of your congregation? If not, you can do some things to change that image.

Recognize the difference between all those whose names are written in the Lamb's "book of life" and the congregations listed in a directory such the one published by the 21st Century Christian – *Churches of Christ in the United States*. The former can be counted only by God while the latter can be counted by mere human beings. There is a difference between the spiritual fellowship of all the saved and the social/historical reality concerning a group of Christians who are similar enough to one another that they see themselves as a group that can be identified by the name "Churches of Christ."

You could start by using once again a slogan that was popular in the early days of the Restoration Movement: "We do not claim to be the only Christians, but we are trying to be Christians only – Christians without prefix or suffix, just plain Christians" – or as we might say today, "generic rather than brand-name Christians." As you do, of course, you will need to recognize that from a sociological and historical perspective, those who are trying to be "Christians only" are a kind of Christian. From a theological perspective what we must consider is whether this is what God would want us to be. The alternative is to accept denominational organizations and division as being a part of God's plan for the church. A few members of the Churches of Christ really do believe that we are the only ones going to heaven. One writer published a tract with the title *Christians Only Are the Only Christians*. But that is the sectarian extreme accepted by only a few.

Teach the difference between the kind of judging we are supposed to do and the kind of judging we are not supposed to do. Teach three forms of judgment to the members of your congregation. Teach it to all who will listen. As you do, you will be addressing an audience that believes in only two alternatives: all who disagree with you are lost – or – others are saved in spite of what you see as serious errors in what they teach and practice. Help people understand a third option: you can teach the truth as you understand it and leave it up to God to do the judging. After all it is really up to God to pass sentence on those who will hear, "I never knew you; depart from me" (Matthew 7:23). We can believe that "Christians Only" is what God would want us to be without passing judgment on those believers who do not share that purpose.

*"We Do Not Believe in Salvation by Grace Through Faith"*

If the people of your community think that members of the Churches of Christ do not believe in salvation by grace through faith, provide positive instruction that helps them see the difference between works of obedience and works of merit. If some members of your congregation believe that grace is the basis of forgiveness for our sins before we are baptized but obedience is the basis of our continued salvation, correct them. Help them to understand the importance of continual Bible study so that we grow in knowledge. Help them recognize the importance of obedience so that we grow day by day to become more like Christ. But teach them that the basis of our continuing salvation is God's grace and not our perfect understanding and perfect obedience. Teach the importance of repenting when we sin so that we do not commit the same sins over and over again. Teach the importance of confessing our sins to God and to those we have wronged. But teach also that we are kept in a saved condition by the perpetual cleansing power of the blood of Christ as long as we do not turn away from him. Model this understanding in public prayers. Instead of always praying, "God, please forgive us for all our many sins," – sometimes say something like, "Thank you, God, that you have already forgiven us."

*"We Do Not Believe We Can Know That We Are Saved"*

Some members of the Churches of Christ need to be better informed on this matter. Something about human pride causes us to think we can earn salvation by the merit of our works if we just try hard enough. When people keep trying and failing, they often conclude that we cannot know for sure that we are in a saved condition. The cure is a correct understanding concerning the doctrine of grace.

We need to point out the error in Calvin's doctrine of "Once Saved, Always Saved." But we need to avoid the opposite extreme: a doctrine of "If Saved, Barely Saved." The kind of teaching needed to correct members of the church who do not understand this matter is exactly the kind of teaching needed to correct a negative image based on the perception that we do not believe we can know we are saved.

*"We Do Not Believe in the Indwelling of the Holy Spirit"*

We do not have to agree on the manner of the Holy Spirit's indwelling to accept the fact that the Holy Spirit really does dwell in Christians. My personal opinions about how the Holy Spirit may guide us, as discussed in Chapter 4, may not be acceptable to some Christians. But we can all accept the fact that divine providence guides us without agreeing on any theory about how this is accomplished. We need to correct those who claim to have miraculous powers or supernatural revelation from God apart from the Bible. But we must never do this in a way that causes Christians to think we have no guidance in the day-to-day affairs of living.

It might be best for us to avoid saying, "The age of miracles is over, and God will not work miracles today." We most certainly should not say, "God cannot work miracles today." We should not limit what God can do. But we can and should point out that some early Christians had miraculous powers to confirm the work that they preached – powers that were given to them by the laying on of the apostles' hands. But when the apostles all died and all those on whom they laid their hands had died, Christians no longer had or needed miraculous powers. According to 1 Corinthians 13:8-10 miraculous gifts of prophecy, tongues and knowledge would pass away "when the perfect comes." Scholars still debate the meaning of the original Greek text for "perfect." But even in the English translations, it is clear that after the miraculous powers would end, "faith, hope, and love" would still remain (v. 13). When Christ returns, faith will be lost in sight and hope will be lost in realization. Only love will abide unchanged. That is why "the greatest of these is love" (v. 13). The language concerning "perfect" may refer to the completion of the New Testament or to the maturing of the church – or to both. But it cannot refer to the return of Jesus Christ at the end of this age as the Pentecostal denominations claim. Clearly the age when some Christians had miraculous powers was to end before the return of Christ. The challenge for Churches of Christ is to teach these things without going to the extreme of denying that the Holy Spirit is active in the world today and especially in the lives of Christians.

*"We Claim That We Do Not Interpret the Bible"*

This was not one of the things mentioned in this study of former members who left Churches of Christ. But it is one that I have encountered. Many years ago the editor of one brotherhood paper wrote an article with the title "We Do Not Interpret the Scriptures." His argument was that members of various denominations interpret the Bible, and their interpretations are the reason for religious division. But he would say that Churches of Christ simply read what the Bible commands and do it. A few personal evangelism training courses have told Christians what to say if someone asks, "How does your church interpret this passage?" The response is supposed to be, "I have no church and if I did it would not be worth joining, but the Lord's church that I belong to does not interpret the Bible. We just read and obey." What is implied here is that "If you could just read the English language correctly, you could read the Bible and you would agree with me."

Some preachers have used the King James Version of 2 Peter 1:20, "no prophecy of the scripture is of any private interpretation," to support their claim that we do not interpret the Scriptures. But even in the King James Version, verse 21 makes it clear that the subject here is the origin of prophecy – not what we do when we read what the prophets wrote. The process of communication, as discussed in Chapter 3, involves interpretation – the attribution of meaning. Without interpretation, there is no communication at all. All of us who read the Bible interpret it. The question is which interpretation is correct.

*"We Do Not All Agree on Every Controversial Issue"*

That is not a misunderstanding. It is a fact. A majority of people in the Churches of Christ would not agree with some of the things I wrote in chapter 7 on "Divorce and Remarriage Issues" or in chapter 11 on "The Role of Women." That does not mean that no truth can be known on these matters. It does not mean that one interpretation is as good as another. It just means that we need to keep on loving one another and keep on studying the Bible and praying for a better understanding of God's will. If we still do not see things alike, we must stay together while we keep on studying and praying. The reason we differ is likely to be that each of us understands a part of God's eternal truth – but we differ because we understand different parts of that truth. The basis of our fellowship in the body of Christ is not our perfect agreement on all doctrinal issues. Instead, it is our common relation with Jesus Christ as Lord and Savior.

Some Christians are thought of as being more "liberal" or "progressive" while others are seen as being more "conservative" or "traditional." Two things are involved in these perceptions: attitudes toward change and matters of conscience. Those who are more progressive favor change while those who are more traditional defend the status quo. We tend to see others as being too liberal if their conscience approves of something that our conscience forbids. We also tend to see others as being too conservative if their conscience forbids something our conscience permits. That, of course, is a very self-centered definition. But in practice, that is how many people use those terms.

In Romans 14:1–15:7, the apostles addressed some issues where Christians differed in matters of personal conscience. Some could eat meat with a clear conscience. Others could not. Some observed certain holy days. Others did not. Paul told the Christians who could not in good conscience eat meat not to judge those who could eat meat without violating their conscience. He told those who ate meat not to look down on those who did not. His conclusion was to "welcome one another as Christ has welcomed you, for the glory of God" (15:7). Christ did not accept us on the basis of our perfect understanding or our perfect obedience. He accepted us because of our acceptance of Him.

## Evangelism

To "close the back door" we need to examine how we are bringing people in the front door. The wrong kind of evangelism is one of the main reasons for a high drop-out rate among new converts.

## Views of Evangelism

In the research that I did for my doctoral dissertation on "Persuasion in Religious Conversion," the churches in which the preacher and the personal evangelism workers accepted a salesmanship view of evangelism had many baptisms but a very low retention rate. Because of this, their net growth rate in regard to adult converts was low. The lowest net growth rate was in congregations where the preachers and personal evangelism workers accepted a teaching model of evangelism. Those churches had few converts, and most of their converts soon dropped out of the church. The best net growth rate was in congregations where the preachers and personal evangelism workers accepted a non-manipulative dialogue model of evangelism in which evangelism is like a conversation with friends.[1]

An evangelistic conversation should not be like a canned sales pitch or a memorized lecture. It should be more spontaneous. Christian evangelists should ask open-ended questions that draw out the understanding and beliefs of the other persons and then really listen with an open mind. Truth has nothing to fear in an open and honest dialogue. Remember there is no room for arguing in an evangelistic dialogue although there is plenty of room for argument. There is an important difference. Arguing involves attacking the opponents and trying to prove that they are wrong. Argument is a logical explanation of what the Christian evangelists believe and why they believe it. That is a gift, not an attack. Argument may also include an explanation of why Christian evangelists cannot see things as the others do. Remember the goal is not to win an argument but rather to win a soul. Soul winning means winning as in a courtship, not winning as in a contest. The purpose is to win the love of others for the Lord Jesus Christ.

Evangelism is the process of influencing others in such a way that Christ in our lives and in our message will be formed in them. Consider what Paul wrote in Galatians 4:19, "[M]y little children, for whom I am again in the anguish of childbirth until Christ is formed in you!"Also consider what Paul wrote about himself. "I have been crucified with Christ. It is no longer I who live, but Christ who lives in me. And the life I now live in the flesh I live by faith in the Son of God, who loved me and gave himself for me" (2:20). What we call "mind," "selfhood," "personality" and "personhood" are developed and sustained in response to significant others in our lives. We identify with them and incorporate them into ourselves. We do not become ourselves by ourselves. If there were no others and no dealing with others, there would be no you. That is how we become fully-functioning autonomous persons. That is also the process by which Christ is formed in us. The power is not in some different and mysterious process. Instead, the power is in Christ. But just as we do not become autonomous persons in response to propositions but rather in response to persons – so it is with Christ being formed in us. That happens in response to the person of Jesus Christ, not in response to propositions concerning doctrines to believe and commands to obey.

## Doctrine-Centered or Christ-Centered?

A major weakness in many approaches to evangelism is that they are doctrine-centered rather than being centered in the person of Jesus Christ. Some focus on preaching the church more than on preaching Christ. One way to correct this problem is to use a narrative rather than a topical approach. Simply tell the story of Jesus. Instead of skipping around from one verse to another and using those verses with little consideration of their context, just tell the story of Jesus. Matthew, Mark, Luke and John are not biographies. They are narrative sermons. That is how the inspired apostles and prophets preached. An approach that some Christian evangelists have found to be very effective is to have conversations with others about Luke and Acts. As you come across verses that talk about doctrines to believe or commands to obey, discuss them. But keep the focus on the person of Christ in Luke and on the work of the Holy Spirit revealing the will of Christ in Acts. A good way to study with unbelievers is to go through John's gospel. Remember the purpose of that gospel: "Now Jesus did many other signs in the presence of the disciples, which are not written in this book; but these are written so that you may believe that Jesus is the Christ, the Son of God, and that by believing you may have life in his name" (John 20:30-31).

This approach to evangelism takes much more time and effort, but those converted in this way are much less likely to drop out of the church. There are, of course, some members of the church who became members of the church in response to a doctrine-centered, church-centered argument and only later really learned about the person of Jesus Christ. Although something was defective in the way they were taught, as they grew day by day they gradually became more and more like Christ. Today it is clear that Christ really lives in them. But that is the exception that proves the rule. For every one who came into the church in that way and still is in the church, probably at least 10 or 20 slipped out the back door.

## Assimilation of New Members

New converts and those who become members of a congregation by transfer of membership from another congregation face some of the same challenges. As a general rule new converts automatically have their names added to a congregation's membership list. Those who transfer membership from another congregation do so by declaring their intention to become members of that congregation. Both processes are called "placing membership" or "being identified" with a congregation as though the two were identical. They are not. Some new converts and some who come by transfer of membership never really become identified with the congregation. Some congregations are not really very accepting with either kind of newcomer. Some individuals make little effort to fit in.

## Friendship Patterns

The more friends new converts make in the congregation the less likely they are to drop out of the church. One study that I did compared 50 new converts who had already dropped out of the church with 50 others who were still attending church services regularly. These two groups were matched by the length of time the people involved were attending church services and in a position to make friends. For example, a drop-out who had attended church services for six months before dropping out was matched statistically with a new convert still attending church services who was interviewed six months after being baptized. One of the things we asked them was how many close personal friends they had in the congregation. All of those who reported having fewer than three friends in the congregation were in the drop-out category. All of those who had more than six friends in the church were in the "faithful convert" category. In between, from three to six, the relationship was very strong. The more friends new converts made in the congregation the less likely they were to leave.[2]

Congregational assessments that I have conducted for more than 100 churches throughout the United States have included anonymous surveys given to the members. One of the questions asked how long they had been attending that congregation. That made a big difference in how they evaluated the congregation. A majority of those who had been attending that church for a long time agreed or strongly agreed with such statements as "This is a warm and friendly congregation" or "This congregation quickly assimilates new members." But a large majority of those who had been members of that congregation for fewer than two years disagreed or strongly disagreed.

Some personal testimony may help to explain this difference in how the newer and older members perceived the congregation. I was a full-time church-supported minister for the first 20 years after my wife and I were married. Part of that time we were involved in domestic church planting ministry in U.S. mission field states. These efforts started with only a few members. It was not hard to break into existing friendship circles. But part of that time we were working with congregations that had 250 to 500 members. In those churches it still was not very hard for us to be accepted, at least partially, into existing friendship circles. I said "at least partially" for a reason. It is easy for the new preacher and his wife to be accepted to a degree but hard for them to establish really close personal relationships. All too often the preacher and his wife are viewed as the "hired help." Furthermore, my father told me that preachers have to be very careful about getting too close to some people to the point that others feel neglected.

In 1973 everything changed. I accepted a position as chairman of a small Speech Communication Program at the University of Tulsa. When we placed membership with a local congregation, we no longer had the "clergy" aura. We found what it was like for "ordinary members" to move into a new congregation and try to make friends. It was not as easy. Then in 1983 we moved to Abilene, Texas, where I had an "in residence" position at Abilene Christian University. Bible professors had something of the "clergy" aura, but I was just a "Researcher in Residence." When we had academic processions, the missionaries-in-residence and I tried to out-humble one another and see who would be at the very end of the line. We lined up by academic rank. The full professors went first, followed by associate professors, assistant professors, lecturers and adjuncts, with the in-residence people bringing up the rear. It was even easier to be humble about our academic positions when it came time to collect our paychecks. All of us who had in-residence positions received one dollar per year from ACU and had to raise our own support. Other than a graduate course in church growth, my only teaching assignments were one-hour short courses. I am not complaining just explaining why my wife and I had very little of the "clergy" aura when we moved to Abilene.

We visited many of the Churches of Christ in Abilene, and they were not very friendly toward visitors. In one of the largest congregations, no one spoke to us unless we spoke first. We finally decided to place membership with the Hillcrest congregation – not because they were all that friendly to visitors and newcomers; they were the least unfriendly. What we observed at Hillcrest was a very warm and friendly congregation with those who were already established members. One time my wife and I stood at the back of the auditorium, and I said, "Look at all that hugging and kissing. It looks like this is a very friendly place." My wife replied, "I wish that we could get in on some of that." A couple standing next to us had recently joined the ACU faculty. The husband said, "You seem to have noticed the same thing we did." We went out to the Dairy Queen for a cup of coffee with them and had a nice visit. Later I became a deacon working in the Involvement Ministry at Hillcrest and did a congregational assessment. My recommendation to the elders was that they should not try to break up the existing friendship circles. I said that they should just try to sanctify those that were too much like cliques. I also recommended that they encourage the new members to form friendship circles among themselves. Following the wise counsel of Lyle Schaller I recommended that they try to get at least one old timer into the new friendship circles to "legitimize" the new groups. The old timers might say, "I am not sure about those newcomers, but they must be okay because Brother Old Timer is a part of that group." Schaller said that if you do not get some mix of old timers and newcomers, you could end up with a range war between the settlers and the squatters.[3] As it turned out, we had a small group that met in homes on Sunday evenings and most of the members of that group either moved to Abilene at the same time we did or had just transferred membership and had become members at Hillcrest at the time we did.

In the summer of 1990, Dr. Carl Mitchell, dean of the College of Bible and Religion at Harding University, offered me a position as a Bible professor. Now I almost had that "clergy" aura again. But before we left Abilene, someone who had just moved to ACU from Harding said to me, "When you get to Searcy, you will find the same thing you found at Abilene. You will be very lonely for the first year or two, and no one will seem to care." That is exactly what we found. We placed membership with the College Church of Christ and found it to be a very warm and friendly congregation – with those who were already included in friendship circles – but not very welcoming toward visitors and newcomers.

Social scientists have found that the average person can handle no more than about seven really close interpersonal relationships at any one time in their life. Those like me who score as introverts on the Myers-Briggs Type Indicator generally have fewer but deeper relationships. Extraverts have more relationships, but they may not be quite as deep. What happens in many congregations is that most of the older members have already met their quota of close personal relationships and are not as motivated to welcome newcomers. The bottom line is that churches need to do more to make sure that everyone who wants to make more friends in the church gets included in at least one friendship circle. Some kind of small group ministry is usually a good step in that direction.

In one congregation where I preached, the involvement ministry included a new member orientation program. New members were introduced to the elders and deacons. They were told about all the different adult Bible classes and training programs that were available. While that was going on, those working with this program privately contacted church members who had things in common with each new member. They focused on characteristics known to be related to the formation of friendship bonds. They contacted members in the same age group with special attention to the age of children or the schools the children attended. They called members who had attended the same college, who had the same occupation, or who lived in the same part of town. They asked these members to meet these newcomers and invite them into their homes for a meal or invite them to go out to a restaurant for a meal. They tried to make sure that every time these newcomers attended a church service someone greeted them and extended such an invitation. This process continued until it appeared that the newcomers were getting personally acquainted with several of the members. Obviously, church leaders cannot force people to become friends or pick who their friends will be. But they can create opportunities for the kind of contact that may be a first step toward the formation of friendship bonds.

Some congregations have "Care Groups" organized by geographical zones and have these groups share a pot luck meal several times a year. There are, of course, many purposes for such groups. In some congregations these groups are organized to help coordinate bringing in food to a family in case of a death or illness. Sometimes elders are assigned to different groups to give each elder a more manageable size of group to shepherd. But one of the goals is usually to create opportunities for people to become better acquainted and facilitate the formation of friendship bonds. The more friends new members make in the church the less likely they are to leave the church.

## Involvement in Ministry Activities

Another factor to consider is how quickly new converts and other newcomers get involved in some areas of congregational ministry. Several studies have found that the sooner new converts get involved in some area of ministry they more likely they are to stay in the church. This also applies to members who come into a congregation by transfer of membership. Those newcomers who are not quickly put to work in some area of congregational ministry are far more likely to drop out of the church.

Studying factors associated with involvement levels in congregations has always interested me. I read everything that I could. I tried to apply the lessons I learned in churches where I was preaching. If I had been able to attend a Christian college or university longer than I did, I might have learned more about this in ministry courses. But after three semesters at Abilene Christian College, I became a financial drop-out. I went into full-time local church work at age 19.[4] After that, I attended state universities near wherever I was preaching. But those secular schools did not offer any ministry courses. So I tried to study things that were related in some way to my work in ministry. Seventeen years and six state universities after leaving Abilene Christian College, I finally graduated with a bachelor of arts degree from the University of Houston. By then I had enough credit hours for a double major in psychology and speech communication with minors in English, history and sociology – but not in Bible or ministry. That may explain the approach I have taken to the church-related research I have done.

The first time that I did survey research was in a social psychology class when I was a senior at the University of Houston. The survey was a study of congregational size as a factor in the involvement levels of congregations. That study found that involvement as I measured it was very low in very small congregations because they had little going on other than the church services. Churches with 100 to 200 members had the highest average involvement levels. As church size increased beyond the 200 level, the lower the involvement level became. But at that time I was preaching for a church with more than 300 members and had previously preached for a congregation with many more than 500 members. For several years I had tried to help these churches grow larger. So I did not stop with the correlation between size and involvement. I knew that some relatively small congregations had low involvement levels, and a few of the largest congregations had high involvement levels. I wanted to know why.

The Behavior Setting Theory of Roger Barker and his associates pointed me in the right direction.[5] Their studies found that small schools had higher involvement levels than big schools and relatively small communities had higher involvement levels than much larger communities. Their explanation involved the ratio of roles available to be filled to the number of participants available to fill those roles. In my application of their approach, I asked church leaders to count the number of specific roles, tasks, church worker assignments or jobs available to be filled in their congregation. Then I asked them to report the number of members available to fill those roles. That is what I called the "actual role-to-member ratio." The correlation between that ratio and involvement was much stronger than the correlation between congregational size and involvement.

In that study done as a class project in 1969, I had a relatively small sample of church members who reported their perceptions about the number of roles to be filled and the number of members available to fill those roles. That is what I called the "perceived role-to-member ratio." The correlation between that ratio and involvement as I was measuring it was almost perfect.[6] As I have continued to study this matter in more than 100 congregational assessments, I have found a strong positive correlation between how involved the average member reports feeling and both the actual and perceived role-to-member ratios.

If the actual role-to-member ratio is too low, the congregation has an organizational problem. They need to create more roles – not just "busy work" but meaningful work to be done. Church size, however, typically increases much faster than the number of roles. As a result, in many large congregations most of the members have nothing to do other than sit in a pew and put money in the collection plate.[7]

If the perceived role-to-member ratio reported by the members is significantly lower than the actual role-to-member ratio reported by the leaders, the problem is one of communication. Most large congregations have both of these problems. That is why many large congregations today have full-time church-supported involvement ministers. Others at least have involvement ministries led by deacons.

Some of these ministers and ministries have a "magnet" approach. They use ministry fairs, bulletin articles and announcements to publicize the various ways in which members can be involved. Others use a more one-on-one approach with something like career counseling for individual members. My preference is for a combined approach.

When I was the Involvement Ministry deacon at the Hillcrest Church of Christ in Abilene, I taught a new member orientation class called "Discovering Your Gifts and Finding Your Ministries." We started this 13-week series with the theology of gifts. We studied the many passages that picture the church as a body with many different parts that have many different functions. We stressed the point that we do not all have the same gifts, but we all have some gifts. One goal was to help people understand that one way God calls us to serve in different ministries is by the gifts God gives us.

The second part of this class involved using several personality inventories. My favorite, as you probably have noticed by now, is the Myers-Briggs Type Indicator. But I also used FIRO-B and FIRO-F. These simple self-report instruments identify the Fundamental Interpersonal Relationship Orientation in regard to Behavior and Feelings: the behaviors and feelings one typically shows to others and wants from them in the areas of inclusion, control and affection. Another instrument useful for this purpose is the Clifton Strengths Finder developed by the Gallup organization.[8] One takes this inventory by first purchasing one of the books that explain the theory and describe 34 different strengths. Each book has an access code for one-time use to take the on-line inventory. The results identify the five top strengths of an individual. These strengths are not directly related to ministries in the church, but they have very clear implications. This instrument is now used by many universities for academic and career counseling.

You might have noticed that I did not mention any of the popular "Gifts Inventories" marketed for use in churches. These are sold to charismatic churches to help identify which members are likely to have gifts for speaking in tongues, casting out demons or healing the sick. Similar inventories are sold to non-charismatic churches to help identify which members are likely to have natural gifts for things such as teaching, preaching, counseling or leadership. The reason I have not used or recommended these Gifts Inventories is that I have never seen one that was properly constructed with tests for internal consistency (split-half reliability) or stability in time (test-retest reliability). They have not been tested for validity. There is no evidence that people identified as having a certain gift actually go on to work in an indicated area of ministry, that they are successful, or that they are satisfied working in that ministry.

The American Psychological Association, the Association for Psychological Type, and several similar professional groups have codes of ethics that prohibit the use of an instrument that does not have published reliability and validity data. I suppose that such Gifts Inventories might be useful as a springboard to conversation about the diversity of gifts. And actually that is the way I have used instruments such as the Myers-Briggs Type Indicator and the Clifton Strength Finder. Neither of these claims to identify directly the specific areas of ministry appropriate for an individual. But they are useful for teaching and counseling purposes. They often get people talking about their giftedness, and that is what is needed.

Getting back to that class on "Discovering Your Gifts and Finding Your Ministries," in the third part of this class, we had each deacon come in and discuss his area of ministry with a focus on how people might get involved. We had enough deacons that we had to have several in each class session. This class was not perfect. It did not always fully achieve its purpose – but it helped.

In another congregation where I preached we used a church worker survey each year. These were much more detailed than those that just list the more obvious roles such as teach a class, lead singing, lead a prayer, read Scripture in the worship assembly or serve as an usher. We asked each deacon to list every role, task, job or function connected with his area of ministry. The elders and ministers added to the list. And we did not just ask the members to check the jobs they were willing to do. We asked for levels of interest. Beside each job description they could check "Very Interested," "Willing," or "No." One year we had 106 items on the list. One of the members checked "No" 105 times. He never checked "Very Interested." The only one where he checked "Willing" was "Donate blood." We had a full-time paid elder in that congregation. He went over all those survey forms. But unlike the deacons who looked for the best people to do the jobs they wanted done, this elder was looking for ways to involve the non-involved members. When he came across the survey form that showed "Donate Blood" as the only thing that brother was willing to do, he immediately called the deacon in charge of the hospital ministry. He explained the situation and asked him to put that brother at the head of the blood donor list. That brother donated blood four times that year and was asked several other times when he could not because it was too soon. The next year when he filled out his church worker survey, he checked several other things. I don't remember whether he still checked "Willing" beside the "Donate Blood" item. But I thank God for elders who are looking for ways to get members more involved instead of just looking for ways to get jobs done. How well a job was done will not make as much difference in eternity as how well people were developed.

## Conclusion

Much more could be said about how to reduce the number of people dropping out of the church. Reading all 325 of these responses has not been easy. In many ways this has been the hardest research I have ever done. It may seem to some who read this book that I have projected my personal beliefs and preferences onto the whole church. If that is what you think, you may be right. Such projecting is a very natural human tendency, and I must admit that I probably do this more than I realize. This kind of thing is much easier to recognize in others than in ourselves. But I would ask you to consider what I have written and accept or reject it on its own merits. Some may think that my reading of Restoration Movement history has been tainted by my personal understanding. But I would respond that if this is not what the pioneers taught, it is what they should have taught. If this is not what they said or how they said it, they should have said it in the way they should have said it.

My father, Flavil R. Yeakley Sr., preached the gospel for more than 60 years. Most of what I learned about ministry I learned from his example or from doing things that did not work and trying to avoid making the same mistakes over and over again. One of the most important lessons I learned from my father and his ministry was this: We must never let the reality of problems in the church-as-it-is blind us to the possibilities of the church-as-it-ought-to-be and to the church it-can-become.

# Endnotes

## Chapter 1

1 The little "c" "church of Christ" is what one reads about in the Bible. It is the spiritual fellowship of all the saved on earth and in heaven. The Big "C" 'Church of Christ," or "Churches of Christ," is what one reads about in the Yellow Pages, a directory, almanac or yearbook. It is a social/historical reality concerning a group of Christians who are similar enough to one another that they see themselves as a group that can be identified by a name. As a church statistician, I study the Big "C" "Churches of Christ." I do so, however, with the understanding that anything humans can count is not the same as the Lamb's "book of life" (Philippians 4:3; Revelation 21:27; 3:5). In the following pages, you will see various religious groups identified as "Christian." That does not mean that I have judged the people in these groups to be saved. It just means that I leave the judging up to God and until then, I just call people what they want to be called. The groups that here are called "Christian" are not Jewish, Muslim, Buddhist or something else. That is all that is implied.

2 Carl H. Royster (compiler), *Churches of Christ in the United States*, 2009 Edition (Nashville: 21st Century Christian) 23.

3 Some of the following material was published earlier in a booklet, *Good News and Bad News: A Realistic Assessment of Churches of Christ in the United States* 2008.

4 Dale E. Jones and others, *Religious Congregations and Membership in the United States 2000* (Nashville: Glenmary Research Center, 2002) 4.

5 *Rhetorical Strategies Analyzed by Social Movement Theory as Applied to Conflict Within the Restoration Movement* (Unpublished M.A. Thesis, University of Houston, 1972).

6 Terry F. Pettijohn, *Psychology: A Concise Introduction*, Third Edition (Sluice Dock, Guilford, Connecticut: The Duskin Publishing Group, 1992) 348-351. See also: Ezra Stotland and Lance K. Canon, *Social Psychology: A Cognitive Approach* (Philadelphia: Lippincott, 1966) 388-394; and Peter B. Warr and Christopher Knapper, *The Perception of People and Events* (London: John Wiley & Sons, 1968) 241-253.

7 H. Richard Niebuhr, *The Social Sources of Denominationalism* (Hamden: Shoe String, 1929). David O. Moberg, *The Church as a Social Institution* (Englewood Cliffs: Prentice-Hall, 1962). Moberg summarizes the study by Liston Pope, *Millhands and Preachers* (New Haven: Yale University Press, 1942). Still earlier, distinguishing characteristics were discussed by Ernst Troeltesh in *The Social Teaching of the Christian Churches*, translated

by Olive Wyan (London: George Allen and Unwin, 1931). Troeltesch said that he received inspiration for the sect-church distinction from Mac Weber. See: Hans H. Geuth and C. Wough Mills, *From Max Weber: Essays in Sociology* (New York: Oxford University Press, 1946) 287-288, 305-306, 313-319. See also: J. Milton Yinger, Religion in the *Struggle for Power* (Durham: Duke University Press, 1946) 19-26, 219-227. For applications of the sect-to-denomination format to Churches of Christ, See: Don Haymes, "The Road More Traveled: How Churches of Christ Became a Denomination," Mission Journal 20 (March 1987) 4-8; and Richard T. Hughes, *Reviving the Ancient Faith: The Story of Churches of Christ in America* (Grand Rapids: Eerdmans, 1996) 2.

## Chapter 2

1 Jeremy E. Uecker, Mark D. Regnerus and Margaret L. Vaaler, "Losing My Religion: The Social Sources of Religious Decline in Early Adulthood," in *Social Forces*, Vol. 85, No. 4, June 2007 (The University of North Carolina Press).

2 Bernard Quinn and others, *Churches and Church Membership in the United States,* 1980 (Atlanta: Glenmary Research Center, 1982). Martin B. Bradley and others, *Churches and Church Membership in the United States*, 1990 (Atlanta: Glenmary Research Center, 1992). Dale E. Jones and others, *Religious Congregations and Membership in the United States 2000* (Nashville: Glenmary Research Center, 2002).

3 Church statisticians use the term "adherents" to include all of the full, confirmed, communicant members plus their children who attend church services but who are not yet baptized or not yet confirmed. It is an estimate of the total church family.

4 Donald A. McGavran, *Understanding Church Growth* (Grand Rapids: Eerdmans, 1970).

5 U.S. Religious Landscape Survey, Pew Forum on Religion and Public Life, Washington: Pew Research Center, 2008) 5.

6 U.S. Religious Landscape Survey 5.

7 Royster ix: provides the following background concerning the work of Mac Lynn as the source of the data published now by the 21st Century Christian: "Part of the earlier data was published by Firm Foundation Publishing House in three editions of *Where the Saints Meet* (1983, 1984, 1987). Other portions were released through an occasional publication called the *Missions Bulletin* (1977-1987), published by the Church of Christ at White Station and the Ross Road Church of Christ, both of Memphis, Tenn. ... Two new volumes

appeared under the titles *Churches of Christ around the World* (Gospel Advocate 1990) and *Churches of Christ in the United States* (Gospel Advocate 1991); the latter was reissued in 1994 by Morrison and Phillips Associates. The 1997 edition of *Churches of Christ in the United States* was published by 21st Century Christian, who followed this with the publication of the 2000 and 2003 editions. ... The 2006 edition represented the first since the transfer of responsibilities [from Mac Lynn to Carl Royster]. This, the 2009 edition, is the latest in a continuing effort for new releases of *Churches of Christ in the United States* to occur every three years."

8 Royster 18.

9 U.S. Census Bureau, *Statistical Abstract of the United States 2006*, Table 52, "Marital Status of the Population by Region."

10 Dale E. Jones regional summaries by Census Bureau Regions: 5-13; and maps showing distributions of: Assemblies of God 542; Church of God (Cleveland, Tenn.) 546; Churches of Christ 549; Seventh-day Adventist Church 556; Southern Baptist 557, 562-563.

11 Dale E. Jones 1-4.

12 David K. Lewis, Carley H. Dodd and Darryl L. Tippens, *The Gospel According to Generation X* (Abilene: ACU Press, 1995).

13 "Factors Associated With Retention Rates Among Young People in Churches of Christ" (Abilene: ACU, 1985).

14 Data on the 5,000 young people in the 100 cluster sample used in the study for the Christian Higher Education Foundation. Also in the sample of campus ministers included in the CHEF study and a *Christian Chronicle* quotation from Lynn Stringfellow, a campus minister from Florida.

15 The part about the return of drop-outs after they get married and have children is based on a smaller sample, more than 100 churches where I have conducted congregational assessments in the past 40 years. In those church studies I asked leaders to make a list of all the young people who grew up attending that church and then find out what happened to them. Frankly, that data base is not as good as I would like it to be. However, I would say that the best educated guess at this point is that 85 percent of those who do not attend a Christian college or university drop out as soon as they leave home, but enough of them come back later in life so that the ultimate drop-out rate is around 50 percent.

16 William D. Hendricks, *Exit Interviews: Revealing Stories of Why People Are Leaving the Church* (Chicago: Moody Press, 1993).

17 Those who accept Calvin's doctrine of "Once Saved Always Saved" use (or misuse) this verse to support their view that those who leave never were

genuine Christians. But this passage does not say that those who left never had been true believers. It just says that by the time they left they were no longer really a part of the Christian fellowship.

## Chapter 3

1 John Stewart (ed), *Bridges Not Walls* (Reading, Mass.: Addison-Wesley, 1982) 8.

2 Roger Shattuck, T*he Forbidden Experiment: The Story of the Wild Boy of Aveyron* (New York: Farrar Straus Giroux, 1980) 5.

3 Stewart 9.

4 John Trent and Gary Smalley, *The Blessing* (New York: Pocket Books, 1986).

5 Martin Buber, "I and Thou," Translated by Ronald Gregor Smith (New York: Charles Scribner's Sons, 1958).

6 See Flavil R. Yeakley Jr., (ed), *The Discipling Dilemma: A Study of the Discipling Movement Among Churches of Christ* (Nashville: Gospel Advocate, 1988).

7 Eric Berne, *Transactional Analysis in Psychotherapy* (New York: Grove Press, 1961); *Principles of Group Treatment* (New York: Oxford University Press, 1964); *Games People Play* (New York: Grove Press, 1964). But a much better way to start, in my opinion, is by reading Muriel James and Dorothy Jongeward, *Born to Win* (Reading: Addison-Wesley, 1971).

8 For a discussion of manipulation and the need for evangelism to be a non-manipulative dialogue, see: Flavil R. Yeakley Jr., *Why Churches Grow*, 3rd ed. (Nashville: Christian Communications, a division of the Gospel Advocate, 1986); and the doctoral dissertation on which this book was based, "Persuasion in Religious Conversion (Unpublished dissertation, University of Illinois, 1975).

9 Berne, *Games People Play.*

## Chapter 4

1 This list shows how many went to other religious groups.

17 - Baptist (Southern Baptist Convention)
13 - United Methodist Church
8 - Roman Catholic
7 - Episcopal Church
6 - Christian Church (Disciples of Christ)
4 - Evangelical Free Church
4 - Presbyterian Church (USA)

2 - Assemblies of God
3 - Reformed Church in America
3 - Unitarian Universalist Fellowship
2 - Baptist General Convention
2 - Eastern Orthodox Church
2 - Vineyard
1 - Church of God (Anderson, Ind.)
1 - Christian and Missionary Alliance
1 - Congregational Church
1 - Cumberland Presbyterian Church
1 - Evangelical Lutheran Church in America
1 - Free Will Baptist Church
1 - International Churches of Christ
1 - Messianic Jews
1 - Plymouth Brethren
1 - said that he stays home and watches Joel Osteen on television

2 James Leslie McCary, *Human Sexuality: Physiological and Psychological Factors of Sexual Behavior* (Princeton: D. Van Norstrand, 1967).

3 McCary 273.

## Chapter 5

1 The first place where I read this three-part outline was in George G. Hunter III, *The Contagious Congregation: Frontiers in Evangelism and Church Growth* (Nashville: Abingdon, 1979). But Hunter and I are both former presidents of the American Society for Church Growth and at one of our meetings he told me that this three-part outline was not his original work – he just did not remember where he read it first.

2 Flavil R. Yeakley Jr., "Persuasion in Religious Conversion," doctoral dissertation (Urbana, Ill.: University of Illinois, 1975). See also: Yeakley, *Why Churches Grow.*

3 C. Peter Wagner, *Your Church Can Grow: Seven Vital Signs of a Healthy Church* (Ventura: Regal, 1976).

4 See C. Kirk Hardaway, *Church Growth Principles: Separating Fact from Fiction* (Nashville: Broadman, 1991).

5 Allan W. Wicker, "Assimilation of New Members in a Large and a Small Church," *Journal of Applied Psychology*, Vol. 55, No. 3, pp. 151-156. See also, Wicker, "Size of Church Membership and Member's Support of Church Behavior Settings," *Journal of Personality and Social Psychology*, Vol. 13, 1969, 278-88; and Wicker, "Organization Size and Behavior Setting Capacity as Determinants of Member Participation," *Behavioral Science*, Vol. 17, 1972,

499-513. In addition to these social science articles, see: Lyle E. Schaller, *The Small Church IS Different!* (Nashville: Abingdon, 1982); and, Carl S. Dudley, *Making the Small Church Effective* (Nashville: Abingdon, 1978).

6 Yeakley, *The Discipling Dilemma* 48-56.

7 Flavil R. Yeakley Jr. *Church Leadership and Organization: A Doctrinal and Practical Study of the Leadership Role of Elders* (Nashville: Christian Communications, Inc., a division of Gospel Advocate, 1986).

8 Karen Hurston, *Growing the World's Largest Church* (Springfield: Chrism, a division of Gospel Publishing House, 1994).

9 "History," Yoido Full Gospel Church "The Tent Church" <http://english.fgtv.com/yoido/history.htm> Accessed 12/9/11.

10 Yoido Full Gospel Church, Organization, "Status of Pastors," <http://english.fgtv.com/yoido/organization.htm.>

## Chapter 6

1 The name and location of the congregation was mentioned in the essay response, but these are omitted here to keep the identity of this person anonymous.

2 Donald A. McGavran, *Understanding Church Growth* (Eerdmans, 1970) 223ff.

3 Now known as the "Great Commission Research Network."

4 Jung's book, *Psychological Types*, was written in German then translated into English in 1923. But when I discuss this with my students at Harding University, I recommend that they start with something a bit easier to read. Isabel Briggs Myers, *Gifts Differing* (Palo Alto: Consulting Psychologists Press, 1980). Even better is the booklet by Isabel Myers and Linda Kirby, *Introduction to Type*, 6th Edition (Palo Alto: Consulting Psychologists Press, 1994).

5 Myers-Briggs Type Indicator and MBTI are registered trademarks of Consulting Psychologists Press, Palo Alto, Calif.

6 Intuition, obviously, is spelled with the letter "I," but that letter was already used for Introversion. "N" is the first letter sounded in the word "Intuition." So in the MBTI results, the letter "N" stands for Intuition.

7 A nationwide random sample of more than 3,000 individuals was refined to produce the most representative samples of 1,478 males and 1,531 females who took the MBTI.

8 Gordon D. Lawrence, *People Types and Tiger Stripes*, 3rd ed. (Gainesville, Fla.: Center for Application of Psychological Type, 1993) 54-55.

9 Earl Paige, "Finding and Following Your Spiritual Path" (Gainesville, Fla.: Center for Application of Psychological Type, n.d.).

10 Actually I did the original design work and helped in the reliability testing of the Form G Self-Scorable that for more than a decade was the best-selling version of the MBTI and the MBTI was already (and still is) the best-selling personality inventory in the history of psychology.

11 Elizabeth Hirsh, *Introduction to Type and Teams*, 2nd ed. (Palo Alto, Calif.: Consulting Psychologists Press, 2003).

12 Yeakley, *The Discipling Dilemma.*

## Chapter 7

1 *Rhetorical Strategies Analyzed by Social Movement Theory as Applied to Conflict within the Restoration Movement* (University of Houston: 1972). That thesis may be read and downloaded at the "Yeakley Research Library" website: <http://www.pureheartvision.org/csl/Yeakley.aspx>.

2 Matthew Henry. *The Matthew Henry Commentary.* One Volume Edition, (Zondervan, 1961) 7.

3 David Gushee, *Getting Marriage Right* (Grand Rapids: Baker, 2004) 94-100.

4 Gushee 147-171.

## Chapter 8

1 3 John 1:9.

2 See: Ephesians 4:11-16; Romans 12:4-8; 1 Corinthians 12:4-31; 1 Peter 4:10-11.

3 Yeakley, *Church Leadership and Organization* 17-30.

4 Yeakley, *Church Leadership and Organization* 31-39.

5 Jim Sheerer and Charles L. Williams (eds), *Directions for the Road Ahead: Stability and Change among Churches of Christ* (Chickasha: Yeomen Press, 1998) 195-197.

6 Sheerer and Williams 185-197.

7 J.R.P. French and B. Raven, "The Bases of Social Power" in D. Cartwright (ed). Studies in Social Power (Ann Arbor: Institute for Social Research, University of Michigan, 1959) 150-167. Gyukl and C.M. Falbe, "Importance of Different Power Sources in Downward and Lateral Relations," in Journal of Applied Psychology, Vol. 76 (1991) 416-423.

8 Yeakley, in Sheerer and Williams, 194. See also: Tom Yokum, "A Word Study on Church Leadership" in Jerry Jones, *What Does the Boston Movement Teach?* Vol. I, 193-199.

9 Fred Craddock, *As One Without Authority* (Nashville: Abingdon, 1971).

# Chapter 10

1 The explanation for the name change given on the church's website is that the church building is actually located in North Richland Hills rather than Richland Hills and the church is expanding to a second location in West Fort Worth so the church will have two meeting places under the supervision of one eldership. More recently the Southlake congregation agreed to work under the supervision of that same body of elders. That one church would then have three "campuses." That is why they needed a more generic name.

2 Carl H. Royster (compiler), *Churches of Christ in the United States* (Nashville: 21st Century Christian, 2006) 31. The Richland Hills Church of Christ located in North Richland Hills, Texas, had an average attendance of 4,000 with 6,414 members and 8,983 adherents.

3 Christian Chronicle. Vol. 69, No. 2, 7.

4 This is the informal fellowship of independent churches that started using instrumental music in the late 1800s but that did not join the Christian Church (Disciples of Christ) when that denomination was organized in the 1950s. In some parts of the country these congregations use the "Christian Church" designation. In other parts of the country they use the "Church of Christ" designation. The directories produced by College Press and by Standard Publishing Company use the combined designation, Christian Churches and Churches of Christ. In 2000 this group was reported to have 5,471 congregations with 1,156,699 members and 1,439,251 adherents. See Dale E. Jones and others, *Religious Congregations and Membership in the United States* 2000 (Nashville: Glenmary Research Center, 2002). p. 1, Table 1: Religious Congregations by Group for the United States: 2000.

5 James William McKinnon, *The Church Fathers and Musical Instruments,* an unpublished doctoral dissertation at Columbia University, 1965, 105-110. According to McKinnon, the absence of instrumental music was not just because playing an instrument would violate Sabbath rules. See Everett Ferguson, *A Cappella Music in the Public Worship of the Church* (Abilene, Texas: Biblical Research Press, 1972) 36, where Ferguson writes, "The real reason for this absence is probably that advanced by McKinnon, namely that the instrument was simply irrelevant to the type of worship developed in the synagogue. It was a non-sacrificial worship and a rational service to which, as an extension either of prayer or of reading the Scriptures, has been added the chanting of the Psalms."

6 Ferguson 81.

7 Thomas C. Alexander, *Music in Worship: A New Examination of an Old Issue* (Nashville: Gospel Advocate, 2010).

8 Of special interest are the following:

Everett Ferguson, *The Church of Christ: A Biblical Ecclesiology for Today* (Grand Rapids: Eerdmans, 1996).

Everett Ferguson, *A Cappella Music in the Public Worship of the Church*, 3rd ed. (Fort Worth: Star Bible, 1999).

Bill Flatt, ed., *The Instrumental Music Issue* (Nashville: Gospel Advocate, 1987).

Milo Hadwin, "What Kind of Music Does God Want?" in *Directions for the Road Ahead: Stability and Change*.

Jimmy Jividen, *Worship in Song: A Study in the Practice of Singing in the New Testament With Implications for Contemporary Worship in Song* (Fort Worth: Star Bible, 1987).

9 The first quotation, from Deuteronomy 6:4-5 (NKJV), came to be known as the *Shema*, named after the first word: "Hear, O Israel: The LORD our God, the LORD is one! You shall love the LORD your God with all your heart, with all your soul, and with all your strength." This passage is quoted by pious Jews every morning and evening. To this day it begins every synagogue service. The other quotation, "[L]ove your neighbor as yourself," came from Leviticus 19:18. This was not second in importance. Jesus said, "On these two commandments hang all the Law and the Prophets" (Matthew 22:40 NKJV). The two tie for first place.

10 Most members of the Churches of Christ are unaware of this history in the Christian Churches. A good example is Stephen J. Corey, *Fifty Years of Attack and Controversy* (Des Moines, Iowa: The Committee on Publication of the Corey Manuscript, 1953). This was written from the perspective of those who became the Christian Church (Disciples of Christ). For a view from the perspective of the Christian Churches that remained independent, see: Edwin V. Hayden, *Fifty Years of Digression and Disturbance* (Joplin: Hunter Printing Company, n.d.).

11 Alfred T. DeGroot, *The Grounds of Division Among the Disciples of Christ* (Chicago: by the author, 1940).

Enos E. Dowling, *The Restoration Movement* (Cincinnati: Standard Publishing Company, 1964).

Winfred E. Garrison and Alfred T. DeGroot, *The Disciples of Christ: A History* (St. Louis: The Bethany Press, 1964).

David Edwin Harrell Jr., *Quest for a Christian America* (Nashville: Disciples of Christ Historical Society, 1966).

James DeForest Murch, *Christians Only* (Cincinnati: Standard Publishing Company, 1962).

12 *Rhetorical Strategies Analyzed by Social Movement Theory as Applied to Conflict With the Restoration Movement* (University of Houston, 1972).

13 See the Abilene Christian University website: www.acu.edu. Also, instrumental-praise small group chapel services are described in the Sept.1, 2010, *ACU Optimist* article "Small group chapels offer unique experiences" by Alan Cherry: <http://www.acuoptimist.com/2010/09/small-group-chapels-offer-unique-experiences/> Accessed 1/19/2012.

## Chapter 12

1 Yeakley, *Why Churches Grow* 75-81.

2 Yeakley, *Why Churches Grow* 54-55.

3 Lyle E. Schaller, *Assimilating New Members* (Nashville: Abingdon, 1978).

4 Actually, I started preaching when I was 16 years old and a sophomore in high school. After that I preached every Sunday morning and Sunday evening. I taught Bible classes every Sunday morning and often on Wednesday evening. By the time I enrolled at Abilene Christian College, I already had more preaching and teaching experience than most of our students today have when they graduate from college.

5 Roger Barker and P. V. Gump, eds. *Big School, Small School: High School Size and Student Behavior* (Stanford: Stanford University Press, 1964). See also: Allan W. Wicker, "Size of Church Membership and Members' Support of Church Behavior Settings." *Journal of Personality and Social Psychology* 11 (1969): 278-288.

6 Dr. Jesse Delia, chair of my dissertation committee at the University of Illinois, helped me understand why that correlation was almost perfect. The percentage of members having a specific church work assignment was one of the elements in my operational definition of congregational involvement, and that was also what I was calling both the actual and the perceived role-to-member ratios. So in effect, I was correlating a number with itself.

7 Yeakley, *Why Churches Grow* 40-45.

8 Donald O. Clifton and Edward "Chip" Anderson with Laurie A. Schreiner, *StrengthQuest*, Second Edition (New York: Gallup Press, 2006). See also: Tom Rath, *Strengths Finder* (New York: Gallup Press, 2007) and Tom Rath and Barry Conchie *Strengths Based Leadership* (New York: Gallup Press, 2008).

CPSIA information can be obtained
at www.ICGtesting.com
Printed in the USA
LVOW10s0506270317
528571LV00015B/242/P

9 780892 255931